12 MONTHS OF FUN!

THE LOBSTER KIDS' GUIDE TO EXPLORING CALGARY

BY KATE ZIMMERMAN
WITH DIANE THUNA

Lobster
Press
Limited

Zimmerman, Kate, 1958-
Thuna, Diane, 1967-
The Lobster Kids' Guide to Exploring Calgary: 12 Months of Fun!

Published by
Lobster Press Limited
1250 René-Lévesque Blvd. West, Suite 2200
Montréal, Québec H3B 4W8
Tel. (514) 989-3121, Fax (514) 989-3168
www.lobsterpress.com

Publisher: Alison Fripp
Editor: Bob Kirner
Senior Editor: Kathy Tompkins
Assistant Editor: Alison Fischer
Production Manager: Allison Larin
Proofreader: Frances Purslow
Cover and Illustrations: Christine Battuz
Icons: Christiane Beauregard and Josée Masse
Layout and Design: Olivier Lasser

Canadian Cataloguing-in-Publication Data
Includes index.

Biennial.
[2000]-
(The Lobster kids' city explorers series)
"12 months of fun!"
ISSN 1493-793X
ISBN 1-894222-0803 (2000 issue)

1. Family recreation—Alberta—Calgary—Guidebooks. 2. Children—Travel—Alberta—Calgary—Guidebooks. 3. Amusements—Alberta—Calgary—Guidebooks. 4. Calgary (Alta.)—Guidebooks. I. Title: Lobster Kids' Guide to Exploring Calgary. II. Series.

FC3697.18.L6 917.123'38043 C00-900422-X
Printed and bound in Canada

This book is dedicated to my intrepid daughter, Zoë and my joyful son, Jake, whose enthusiasm for the project was boundless. Their friends helped a lot, too: Jackson Chase, Chloë Ciancio, Ashley Eastgaard, Carla Dalgleish, Alana Hornby, Brittany King, Jonny Linton, Henry Mason, Sam Mason, Graham Mayes, Taryn Presseau, Carolyn Rowan and Christopher and Cody Shearer. My thanks go to Valerie Fortney, who recommended me, to Brian Mason, for his warm encouragement, and to Alison Mayes, for being a great sounding board and information source. I'd also like to thank Ron Shewchuk, my constantly supportive, always sunny husband and ally.

Diane Thuna was a godsend, or, more accurately, a Bob-send, since she was found by our marvellous, patient editor at Lobster, Bob Kirner. We couldn't have done this Lobster Guide without the help of Calgary Transit and Calgary Parks and Recreation. Many thanks go to Calgary writer and cookbook author dee Hobsbawn-Smith, who provided us with vital information. Our thanks also go to Lobster's superbly organized and cheerful Alison Fischer, as well as all the others at Lobster, including Publisher Alison Fripp, whom we never got to meet but who supported us all the way.

Thanks and Merci!

KATE ZIMMERMAN

I would like to dedicate this book to my son, Sean, my constant and delightful companion in this endeavour and to my husband, Garry, without whose enthusiasm and support I would be lost. Grateful thanks also go to fellow writers Drew McKibben and Diane Bailey who recommended me for this project.

DIANE THUNA

Table of Contents

Author's Introduction

What a vital, interesting place Calgary has become! The town that sprang up in the 1880s around a bunch of renegade whisky traders has matured into a sprawling city whose history, culture, economy and proximity to the wilderness draws tourists from all over the world.

This maturity has also meant growth in the area of amusing and educating families—which, of course, is the subject of this book. In researching this Lobster guide, we've discovered a vast array of activities geared toward children and the adults they let tag along with them.

Who can resist the allure of horseback riding in the foothills, biking city trails, racing go-carts or dashing through the snow on a dogsled? Thankfully, when the temperature dips below minus 20 Celsius, the city is also well equipped with wave-pools, climbing walls, pottery and soap-making workshops and experts in making rain-sticks out of recycled materials. The list goes on and on.

It took detective work to unearth some of the nuggets you'll find here—especially those in the Farther Afield chapter. But we were surprised and excited to find so much happening, and so many institutions and organizations devoted to entertaining children.

Whether you're a visitor to Calgary, a teacher on a quest for worthwhile field trips, or a local family with a thirst for adventure, this book should prove informative, engaging and, we hope, inspiring. Enjoy your exploration!

KATE ZIMMERMAN

A Word from the Publisher

Lobster Press is proud to present *The Lobster Kids' Guide to Exploring Calgary*, the next in our series of guidebooks that offer information and ideas for exploring Canadian cities with children. We won't keep you long from enjoying this book, but first we want to highlight a few things so you can get the most out of our guide.

Whether you're a parent, a teacher or a tourist, if you're caring for children between the ages of 1 and 12, this book is ideal for you. It's a complete resource of things to do and see with kids in the Calgary area, both indoors and out, through all four seasons and for all budgets.

The sites in this guide were visited in 1999-2000 and the information given for each has been verified. However, since prices and opening hours are liable to change and roads are sometimes under construction and some sites close their doors, please accept our apologies in advance for any inconveniences you may encounter.

Take a moment to read about the "Lobster Rating System." It was created to let you know what Kate and Diane's families thought of each site. Some sites and activities weren't rated because they did not fit all the rating criteria.

Next, familiarize yourself with our icons. We designed them to provide information at a glance and also to give you a smile.

The distances to all the sites and activities were determined from the Calgary Tower. We think it is a good meeting point for east, west, north and south.

We welcome your comments. We couldn't include everything that's available for children in Calgary, so if you feel that we've missed one of your family's favourite destinations, please contact us and we'll print it in the next edition.

A last word: Please be careful when you and your children visit the sites in this guide. Neither Lobster Press, Kate Zimmerman nor Diane Thuna can be held responsible for any accidents you or your family might incur.

Enjoy! And watch for the other six books in The Lobster Kids' City Explorers series: The Lobster Kids' Guides to Exploring Montréal, Ottawa-Hull, Vancouver, Toronto, Halifax and Québec City.

FROM THE GANG AT LOBSTER PRESS

The Lobster Rating System

We thought it would be helpful if you knew what Kate, Diane and their families thought about the sites in this book before you head off to visit them. They rated every attraction and activity they visited for its:

- ☞ enjoyment level for children
- ☞ learning opportunities for children
- ☞ accessibility from the Calgary Tower
- ☞ costs and value for the money

A one-lobster rating: Good attraction.

A two-lobster rating: Very good attraction.

A three-lobster rating: Excellent attraction.

Not fitting some of the criteria, and subsequently not rated, are green spaces and various similar, nearby or other attractions.

Table of Icons

These facilities and/or activities are represented by the following icons:

Beach

Bicycling

Birthday parties

Bus stop

Coat check

Cross-country skiing

Downhill skiing

First aid

Heated chalet

Hiking

Ice cream stand

In-line skating

Information centre

LRT station

Parking

Picnic tables

Playground

Restaurant/snack bar

Skating

Snowshoeing

Swimming

Telephone

Tobogganing

Toilets

Wheelchair/stroller accessible

Wildlife watching

Calgary Transit (CT) recommends that when travelling in the downtown core visitors use the LRT rather than city buses, which are scheduled to be convenient for office workers. Shuttle bus 31 does a circuit through downtown, but it can be a long ride depending on your destination. For information about shuttle frequency and places to board, visit www.calgarytransit.com or call (403) 262-1000 during non-business hours.

Getting Ready

Once you've planned an activity for the day, why not take a few minutes and prepare for it. Nothing will ruin an outing faster than forgetting something important at home. These helpful suggestions will ensure your next trip is pleasant for everyone.

☞ Call ahead and verify the site's opening hours and prices.

☞ If you're travelling a considerable distance, pack healthy snacks for everyone.

☞ Remember to bring along liquids.

☞ Pack a road map and a first-aid kit, and be sure that anyone who is taking medication has it with them.

☞ Does anyone get car sick? Bring the Gravol™.

☞ Playing "I Spy," having singsongs and listening to your kids' favourite cassettes while on the road will make the drive more pleasant and delay the inevitable "Are we there yet?"

☞ You already know about packing diapers, wipes and spare clothes. But remember to pack a small toy or two for the baby to play with.

☞ Coloured pencils and scratch pads keep little hands busy on a long drive and while waiting for a restaurant meal.

☞ If you're visiting a park, bring along a Frisbee™, a Hacky Sack™ or a soccer ball.

☞ After a long car ride, take the children to a park before heading to a museum or similar site.

☞ Pack insect repellent, sunscreen, swimsuits, towels and hats if it's summer and you're going to an outdoor site.

☞ Bring extra hats, gloves, scarves, boots and warm coats for outdoor winter activities. Dress in layers, wearing a polycotton or other moisture-releasing fabric next to your body. A dab of Vaseline™ applied to cheeks and noses reduces the risk of frostbite—so can running to the nearest canteen for hot chocolate!

☞ This book uses the metric system, where distance is measured in kilometres, height in centimetres, weight in kilograms and area in hectares. Temperature is measured in centigrade. For those unfamiliar with these units:

→ One kilometre is just over a half mile (0.62 mile).

→ For certain midway rides and waterslides the minimum height requirement is 122 centimetres or four feet.

→ One kilogram is equivalent in weight to just over two pounds (2.2 pounds).

→ One hectare is approximately the same area as two and a half acres (2.47 acres).

→ Water freezes at 0°C (32°F). When the temperature's 25°C (77°F) it's shorts and T-shirt weather.

Bon voyage!

Getting Around with Young Children

Some of the sites in this guide are located on expansive grounds and are only accessible on foot. This may be problematic for parents with children in strollers, especially if the walk is over rough terrain. In this guide, sites indicated as being wheelchair accessible are suitable for strollers as well.

Transporting Babies

Instead of using a stroller, you might consider carrying your child in a Snugli™. When babies grow out of their Snuglies™ and can hold their heads up properly, they're old enough to be transported in child carrier backpacks. Backpacks are ideal for all types of terrain.

Bicycling with Children

Today, more and more parents want to include their children on long-distance bicycle rides. If your kids are too young to ride on their own, you can carry them in children's bike seats or in a trailer or trail-a-bike. Used alone or in combination, these accessories provide safe and worry-free bicycling for the entire family. Remember to fit your children with approved bicycle helmets.

Cross-country Skiing with Small Children

Even if children lack the technique and stamina to cross-country ski, families can still enjoy a day on the trails using one of two devices for carrying them. A carrier backpack is ideal as long as the adult who is wearing it is a strong skier and avoids steep hills. You can also use a ski trailer. Hiking and bicycle shops carry a variety of makes, but keep your eyes open for quality models such as Scandinavia's Ski-pjulken. Though remember, while the skiers in your party are working up a sweat, any youngster who's in a ski trailer is lying in the cold.

Chapter 1

Local Attractions

Introduction

With its erratic foothills weather, Calgary is a city where family activities are very much influenced by temperature and conditions. When the day is cold or wet, people flock to the Science Centre or the IMAX™ Theatre; when it's sunny and warm, they head for Calaway Park or the zoo. However, that's when those places are the most crowded, and the experience is a lot less pleasant when you're lining up for exhibits, food and washrooms.

Try taking the opposite approach occasionally, heading off to Calaway Park when the skies are a little overcast, or ambling through the zoo on a summer's evening with a picnic in tow instead of arriving at noon.

There's plenty to do in these foothills, so you can afford to be choosy. Bombing along the mountain bike trails at Canada Olympic Park is just as refreshing when there's a breeze as when the sun is blazing. A walk through the hustle and bustle of Eau Claire Market is easy and inviting no matter how inclement the weather. Other local attractions for families are Prince's Island Park, the Chinese Cultural Centre and the Calgary Tower. And don't forget the Calgary Stampede, a ten-day city-wide party with its rodeo, square-dancing, and free pancake breakfasts celebrating all that's Western.

The city's your prairie oyster. So, pack a bag with a jacket for everyone just in case the weather changes, and head out for a day of fun.

Creatures Great and Small
THE CALGARY ZOO

1300 Zoo Rd. N.E.
Calgary
(403) 232-9300
www.calgaryzoo.com

Founded in 1929, the Calgary Zoo has grown from a modest spot with few animals to more than 61 hectares of land, buildings and enclosures housing 1,100 feathered, furry and reptilian creatures from all over the world. Besides the ever-popular lions, tigers, gorillas and elephants, the zoo has an Australian/Nocturnal house and a Canadian Wilds section where kids can spy cougars, wolves and owls.

But the animals are only part of the attraction. Prehistoric Park, landscaped to resemble the hoodoo-strewn turf where the dinosaurs once roamed, is punctuated by towering life-size replicas of the beasts. Elsewhere there are playgrounds and facilities for

Seasons and Times

→ Spring and Fall: Apr 3—June 2 and Aug 30—Oct 11, Mon—Fri, 9 am—4 pm; weekends, 9 am—6 pm.
Summer: June 24—Aug 29, daily, 9 am—8 pm.
Winter: Oct 12—Apr 4, daily, 9 am—4 pm.

Cost

→ May 1—Sept 30: Adults $10, children (2 to 17) $5.
Oct 1—Apr 30: Adults $8, children (2 to 17) $4.
Under 2 free. Half price for seniors Tuesday to Thursday, year-round. Memberships available.

Getting There

→ By car, take Memorial Dr. east to the St. George's Dr. turnoff. Follow the signs to the zoo. Free parking at the west gate lot. About eight minutes from the Calgary Tower.

→ By public transit, take CT bus 1 (Forest Lawn/Bowness) to 9th Ave. and 12th St. S.E. Walk north on 12th St. until you reach the east zoo entrance. Or take the LRT (Whitehorn train) to the Calgary Zoo Station and follow the signs.

→ On foot, walk east along 9th Ave. until you reach 12th St., turn north and cross the bridge.

☞ Getting There
➛ By bicycle, use the car directions. Bike racks at the west gate.

☞ Nearby
➛ The Inglewood Bird Sanctuary.

☞ Comment
➛ Stroller rentals ($2). Plan a 3-hour visit.

dining indoors and out, so you can buy your lunch or take a picnic. The Botanical Gardens at the Conservatory, always enticing, feature a rain forest, an arid garden and a butterfly garden that's gorgeous when blooming with fragrant spring flowers.

The zoo stages seasonal events. Call the special events line (232-9353) for information about upcoming festivities. Programs, including stinky but fun group sleepovers in the Large Mammal House, happen regularly.

The Heart of the Action
EAU CLAIRE MARKET

2nd Ave. and 2nd St. S.W.
Calgary
(403) 264-6460
www.eauclairemarket.com

The heart of Calgary's downtown is the Eau Claire Market area, enthusiasts of Olympic Square and Stephen Avenue Mall notwithstanding. In the summer when the weather's fine, Eau Claire's outdoor water park and modest playground attract children of all ages. Its proximity to leafy Prince's Island (page 24) across the Bow River, with its paths for walking and biking and stages for many of the city's festivals, makes Eau Claire a natural hang-out. Whether your family is in-line skating, walking the dog or simply out for a stroll, you'll find buskers performing indoors and out, whatever the season. There are kid-friendly restaurants around the perimeter of the Market building and there's a popular ethnic food fair within.

The Market is also home to the IMAX™ and Cineplex theatres, and the Cinescape Multi-Media Family Entertainment Centre (265-4511) with its sophisticated arcade games, simulated roller-coaster ride and Internet Café. Who's Who in the Zoo, a store that specializes in wind-up toys, is a big hit with youngsters. So is the ice cream store and the candy shop.

☞ SEASONS AND TIMES

➛ Market: Mon—Wed, 10 am—6 pm; Thu—Fri, 10 am—9 pm; Sat—Sun, 10 am—6 pm.
Water park: June—Sept, daily, 9 am—10 pm (weather permitting, call 268-2300).

☞ COST

➛ Free.

☞ GETTING THERE

➛ By car, take 9th Ave. east to Macleod Trail, turn north to 4th Ave. and go west. Proceed to 2nd St. S.W. Turn north to 2nd Ave., then head west. Pay parking on site and on nearby streets. About eight minutes from the Calgary Tower.

➛ By bus, take CT bus 31 (downtown shuttle; see note page 14). By LRT, take the City Centre train and get off at 7th Ave. and 2nd St. Walk north along 2nd. The market will be in front of you.

➛ By bike or on foot, go west on 9th Ave. until 2nd St. and head north to the market.

☞ NEARBY

➛ Eau Claire YMCA, Prince's Island, Chinatown, Calgary Tower, Stephen Avenue Mall, Olympic Plaza.

☞ COMMENT

➛ Plan a 2 to 3-hour visit if Prince's Island, the Market and the water park are in store.

Jewel on the Bow
PRINCE'S ISLAND PARK

1st Ave. and 4th St. S.W.
Calgary
(403) 268-3888
www.gov.calgary.ab.ca
(search under parks and recreation)

Smack dab in the middle of the Bow River, Prince's Island is a lovely, clean, green spot that's only accessible on foot or by bike. There's a fine walking path for families who want to take it slow and easy, though 'bladers are welcome, too. The rocky shore of the island, to the north, is fun for children to explore (with watchful supervisors). A playground is popular with kids, as is watching the local wild ducks and Canada geese. Summertime sees free performances of a variety of plays under the banner of Shakespeare in the Park. A lagoon with a splendid fountain and sports fields round out the area's attractions.

Prince's Island is the site of many of Calgary's biggest and best festivals, including the Folk Fest

Seasons and Times

➛Year-round: Daily, 6 am—10 pm. Hours extended during festivals.

Cost

➛ Park: Free.
Festivals: Varies.
Shakespeare in the Park: Donations accepted.

Getting There

➛By car, take Centre St. north to 2nd Ave. Turn west and continue to 2nd St. S.W. where there's pay parking in the Eau Claire Market area. Walk over the bridge to the island. About ten minutes from the Calgary Tower.

➛ By bus, take CT bus 31 (downtown shuttle; see note page 14) to Eau Claire Market and walk north to the park. By LRT, take the City Centre train and get off at 7th Ave. and 2nd St. Walk north along 2nd. The market will be in front of you. Walk north along Barclay Parade and cross over the bridge to the park.

➛ By bike or on foot, use the car directions.

and CariFest, which usually have an appealing, mellow atmosphere, fine performers and great food kiosks. In early September, Festival on the Bow marries an unlikely duo: classical music and a Southern-style barbecue competition. Pack kids' bathing suits, towels, hats, sunglasses and sunscreen during the summer season for the wading pool at Eau Claire Market, and bring food, drinks and a blanket to spread beneath you. If you're planning to stay for the evening, take sweaters; breezes can suddenly spring up and surprise you.

> **COMMENT**
> → Dogs and bikes are not allowed on-site during festivals. Plan at least a 1-hour visit.

Ups and Downs
CALAWAY PARK

HWY. 1 AND SPRINGBANK RD.
CALGARY
(403) 240-3822
WWW.CALAWAYPARK.COM

Western Canada's largest amusement park operates on the principle that Ma or Pa pays an entry fee for the family's admission and then all the rides are free. Among the over 25 carnival rides at this site west of Calgary are a wild roller coaster, a wet log ride, giant slides, gentle bumper boats, a

> **SEASONS AND TIMES**
> → Spring: May 16—June 21, Fri, 5 pm—10 pm; weekends, 10 am—8 pm.
> Summer: June 22—Aug 31, daily, 10 am—8 pm.
> Fall: Sept 5—Oct 12, weekends, 11 am—6 pm.

☞ Cost
➛ Regular (7 to 49) $18.50, junior (3 to 6) $12.50, 50 plus $10, under 3 free, family of four $50. Each additional family member $10.
Prices include admission and unlimited rides. Group rates available.

☞ Getting There
➛ By car, take Centre St. north to 16th Ave. and drive west for about 15 kilometres. Calaway Park is on your left. Turn off and cross the highway at Springbank Rd. Free parking on site. About 20 minutes from the Calgary Tower.

☞ Nearby
➛ Canada Olympic Park.

☞ Comment
➛ Stroller and locker rentals. Diaper-changing facilities and an ATM are on site. Some rides are wheelchair accessible. Plan at least a 3-hour visit.

haunted house, kiddie cars and trains . . . all set on the prairie in a pseudo-Prehistoric getup that's well-landscaped and clean.

The Fishing Hole allows kids to fish and land a rainbow trout. A nine-hole minigolf course with a western theme also provides a challenge. Live entertainment is presented regularly on the park's musical stages and at its Showtime Theatre. Concessions around the park sell fast food.

Beware the sunny days of summer vacation, when the parking lot is packed and the line-ups are long. Instead, try visiting when the sky is overcast, or go in the off-season. Discount coupon giveaways at gas stations and discount vouchers in coupon books will save you money—Calaway Park is not cheap and the midway games are not free.

Putting the Fun in Science
THE CALGARY SCIENCE CENTRE

701 - 11TH ST. S.W.
CALGARY
(403) 221-3700 (GENERAL INFORMATION)
WWW.CALGARYSCIENCE.CA

Cold or rainy days are busy at the Calgary Science Centre, because it's packed with indoor things to do. The centre does an excellent job of demystifying science and making it fun for everyone with ever-changing interactive exhibits, films on Alberta's largest indoor screen and multimedia presentations. Discovery Hall has all kinds of entertaining exhibitions, which in the past have included Beakman's World on Tour and Thingmajigs: Celebrating Wacky Inventions. Steer kids ages three to seven to Working Wonders, where they'll find digging machines, a playhouse with slides, a crafts centre and costumes for dressing up.

The centre's Outdoor Amazement Park offers children opportunities to learn while they play, using a lever to hoist a 340-kilogram globe and composing tunes on instruments made out of everyday construction materials. Bring your lunch and take advantage of the picnic areas here, or buy

☞ SEASONS AND TIMES

➛ Summer: June 29—Sept 12, Mon—Sun, 9:30 am—5:30 pm.
Fall, Winter, Spring: Sept 13—June 28, Tue—Thu, 10 am—4 pm; Fri—Sun and holiday Mondays, 10 am—5 pm.

☞ COST

➛ Adults $9, youths (13 to 18) and seniors $7, children (3 to 12) $6. Prices are for the regular hours described above and include access to all exhibits and one Discovery Dome show.

Getting There

➛ By car, take Centre St. to 6th Ave. S. Turn west and continue to 11th St. Free parking underneath and beside the Science Centre. About seven minutes from the Calgary Tower.

➛ By public transit, take the City Centre LRT to 10th St. and walk one block to the Centre. Or take CT bus 31 (downtown shuttle; see note page 14).

➛ By bicycle or on foot, go west along 9th Ave. to 11th St., then continue north just past 7th Ave. The Centre is on your left.

Nearby

➛ Eau Claire Market, Prince's Island.

Comment

➛ There are first aid supplies on site, but not personnel. Diaper-changing facilities. Plan a 3-hour visit.

snacks from the kiosk inside.

The Science Centre offers summer camps, birthday packages, curriculum-oriented school programs and other events. Visiting astronauts, astronomers and other kid-friendly scientists regularly give talks. Call the centre or visit its Web site for details.

Look Up, It's the CALGARY TOWER

101 - 9TH AVE. S.W.
CALGARY
(403) 266-7171
WWW.CALGARYTOWER.COM

The thrill of riding the elevator at top speed to the apex of a 190.8-metre tower is reasonably large for kids, but only the older ones will really appreciate how far you can see on a clear day from one of the highest points in the city. Little children won't be able to put the 360-degree panoramic view into context and, within minutes, may well start pestering you for coins for the video games that are scattered around the observation deck.

Their older siblings will be able to play "spot the building" using the photo guides positioned strategically on the deck near $1-per-view stationary binoculars. There are the mountains to the

☞ SEASONS AND TIMES

➛ Year-round: Daily, 8 am–10 pm. Reduced hours on Christmas Day.

☞ COST

➛ Adults $6.15, seniors (65 and older) $4, youths (13 to 18) $4.30, children (3 to 12) $2.95, under 3 free.
Yearly Elevation Passes available.

☞ GETTING THERE

➛ By car, take 9th Ave. west to 1st St. S.W. Drive half a block further west and you are there. Pay parking on site (daily maximum $8).
➛ By public transit, take the City Centre LRT to 1st St. S.W. and 7th Ave. Walk two blocks south to 9th Ave. and half a block east. Or take CT bus 31 (downtown shuttle; see note page 14).
➛ By bicycle, use the car directions.

☞ NEARBY

➛ Stephen Avenue Mall, Arts Centre, Glenbow Museum.

☞ COMMENT

➛ There are diaper-changing facilities on the observation deck; however, bring a changing pad and wipes from home. Plan a 30-minute visit.

west, the Saddledome to the east . . . this is one way for school-age kids, especially newcomers, to get a grasp of the city.

Feel free to take your own food and commandeer a table by the window on the observation deck. There's also a coffee bar and two restaurants if the brief elevator ride leaves your brood peckish. A festive occasion may warrant the Sunday brunch buffet at the top of the Tower. Check out the Elevation Lobby as well for a display depicting towers of the world.

Go for Gold
CANADA OLYMPIC PARK

88 Canada Olympic Rd. S.W.
Calgary
(403) 247-5452 or (403) 521-5222
(code 8925 for special events)
www.coda.ab.ca/cop

The 1988 XV Winter Olympic Games in Calgary left the city a lasting legacy. Among the sites developed for the Games was this 110-hectare hilly spot west of town, which has become a year-round destination for families.

The Olympic Hall of Fame and Museum (page 39) allows kids, via computer simulation, to experience the thrill of hurtling down the Olympic Bobsleigh/Luge Track and soaring through the air off the park's 70-metre ski tower. They can also test their mettle in the interactive Olympic Challenge Gallery and be awarded a virtual medal. No one should miss the rousing Olympic films at the museum's theatre.

Outdoors, there's an 18-hole minigolf course, a playground and Calgary's only full-facility mountain bike park. It boasts 15 kilometres of cross-country trails for beginner, intermediate and advanced riders and there's a dual slalom course. Bring your mountain bikes (rentals and repairs are available), buy a chair lift pass and the trails are yours, year-round. Ski jumping is offered (summer and winter), as well as winter-time skiing (downhill and cross-country) and snowboarding.

Camps in the summer focus on sports adventures and there are mountain bike race leagues, clinics and training for all levels.

☞ SEASONS AND TIMES

→ Summer: May 22—Oct 1, daily, 10 am—9 pm (9 am—9 pm, July and August).
Winter: Mid-Nov—early April, call for conditions.

☞ COST

→ Summer: $6 for chairlift.
Winter ski pass (full day): Adults (18 to 54) $21, youths (13 to 17) $19, children (5 to 12) $12. Partial day rates are available.
Olympic Hall of Fame and Museum: $7 per person (self-guided tour), $10 per person (guided tour), children under 5 free.
Minigolf: Adults $7, students and seniors $6, kids 10 and under $5. Game packs available.
C.O.P. season's passes available.

☞ GETTING THERE

→ By car, take Centre St. to 16th Ave. Drive west for about 15 kilometres until the Canada Olympic Rd. turnoff (look for the ski jump towers on your left). Free parking on site. About 15 minutes from the Calgary Tower.
→ By public transit, CT bus 408 offers limited weekday service to the park. Call 262-1000.
→ By bicycle, C.O.P. is about a 50-minute ride from downtown along City of Calgary trails.

☞ NEARBY

→ Calaway Park.

☞ COMMENT

→ Diaper-changing facilities in the larger washrooms. Plan at least a 2-hour visit.

School Programs (247-5451), birthdays and Sleep Under the Stars sleepovers are all available, and volunteer opportunities for kids 13 and up abound (247-5409).

Exploring Our Asian Roots
CALGARY CHINESE CULTURAL CENTRE

197 - 1st St. S.W.
Calgary
(403) 262-5071
www.culturalcentre.ab.ca

The imposing building at the west end of Chinatown is the Calgary Chinese Cultural Centre, and it's worth passing through its enormous doors to gaze up inside at the seven-storey multi-coloured dome at the Dr. Henry Fok Cultural Hall. The dome features 561 dragons and 40 phoenixes and was modelled on the temple of Heaven in Beijing. For little kids, it—and the four gorgeously decorated red and gold columns in its lobby—might be enough. However, there are art exhibits on the second and third floors, and older children may want to investigate the museum in the basement.

☞ Seasons and Times

➛ Centre: Year-round, daily, 9 am–9 pm.
Museum: Year-round, daily, 11 am–5 pm.

☞ Cost

➛ Centre: Free.
Museum: Adults $2, seniors (65 and older), students (with valid ID) and children (6 to 12) $1, under 6 free.

It's a fairly modest spot, with displays of ancient pottery, clothing and reproductions of interesting artifacts. Life-size terra-cotta soldier replicas, with their horses, monopolize one room and another is devoted to chronicling the struggles of the Chinese who arrived in Calgary in the early 1900s. The museum is strictly narrative and has a formal, serious feeling that will appeal most to those with an interest in Chinese culture.

Upstairs, Chinese-language and history classes are offered at the Calgary Chinese Public School and the Cultural Centre Chinese Learning Academy. An arts and crafts store that carries imported items (including toys), an auditorium and a restaurant also call this building home.

☞ GETTING THERE

➛ By car, by bicycle or on foot, take Centre St. north to 2nd Ave. and turn west. The centre is at the end of the street. Meters and parking lots in the area. About seven minutes from the Calgary Tower.

➛ By public transit, take CT bus 31 (downtown shuttle; see note page 14). By LRT, take the City Centre LRT and get off at Centre St. and 7th Ave. Walk north to 2nd Ave. and west one block to 1st St. S.W.

☞ NEARBY

➛ Chinatown, Eau Claire Market, Prince's Island.

☞ COMMENT

➛ The museum is wheelchair-accessible via the restaurant; call ahead and let them know you will need this access. Plan a 40-minute visit.

After the visit, why not do some exploring around Chinatown? Bakeries and markets there offer all kinds of fresh, inexpensive, delectable delights, sweet and savory.

Whooping it Up THE CALGARY STAMPEDE

1410 Olympic Way S.E.
Calgary
(403) 261-0101
www.calgary-stampede.com

Calgary's annual Exhibition and Stampede can't fail to entertain anyone but the youngest child, who might be put off by the noise, crowds and carny atmosphere of the Stampede Grounds. Other kids are in hog heaven, whether they're testing out the carousel in the Kiddie Corral or thrill-seeking at the Midway proper, roaring around the roller coaster track. What sets the Stampede apart from other Canadian exhibitions, though, is the rodeo, and it's well worth the extra cost of admission. The cowboys and cowgirls are experts in their areas of derring-do, which range from calf-roping and bull-riding to racing chuckwagons at heart-stopping speeds.

☞ Seasons and Times

➛ Early July—Mid-July.
Stampede Grounds: 11 am—midnight.
Grounds open at 9 am on Family Day, Kids Day and other special days. Check the newspapers or Stampede booklet for details.

☞ Cost

➛ General admission: Individuals (13 to 64) $9, seniors (65 and up) and children (7 to 12) $4, under 7 free. Sneak-A-Peek (Thursday night before opening day): 7 and over $4. All-Day Midway Rider vouchers are available at Safeway stores prior to Stampede.
Rodeo tickets range in price from $20 to $40, depending on the location of the seat and which day you attend. For several days of the rodeo, children's tickets in designated sections are half-price. Evening tickets include the nightly Grandstand show and fireworks display.

Among the other child-pleasing attractions you'll find on the grounds are the Indian Village (where colourful teepees dot the grass and accomplished native dancers perform traditional dances) and the Big Top building, where kids can view farm animals and watch blacksmiths competing for world championships. Elsewhere, there are sheep-shearing contests and pig races, craft making, pop and country concerts and much, much more.

The Stampede can get pricey. If money is particularly tight, consider going on Family Day or Kids Day, when there's free admission, live music and a complimentary breakfast for those arriving before 9 am.

The Stampede extends far beyond the park gates. Events held throughout the city during this ten-day festival include square-dancing demonstrations, live country music shows and Stampede Breakfasts with free pancakes and live music. Consult your newspaper for schedules.

And don't forget the Stampede Parade, which takes place downtown on the first Friday morning of Stampede. "Dress Western," then choose your position curbside early armed with lawn-chairs,

☞ GETTING THERE

➛ By car, take 9th Ave. east to 1st St. S.E. and go south until 1st meets Macleod Trail. The Stampede Grounds are on your left. Look for parking on neighbouring streets. About seven minutes from the Calgary Tower.

➛ By public transit, take any LRT to Victoria Park Stampede Station. Or take CT bus 10 (Southcentre), which drops you off at the corner of 1st St. and 17th Ave. S.E. Take the pedestrian walkway over to the park.

➛ By bicycle or on foot, use the car directions. There are bicycle racks at the entrances.

☞ NEARBY

➛ Calgary Tower.

☞ COMMENT

➛ Diaper-changing facilities near the medical stations and Kiddie Corral. Bring a changing pad and wipes. Wheelchair, stroller and locker rentals near the gate entrances. Plan at least a 4-hour visit.

snacks and sunscreen. Spend a happy morning yelling "Yahoo!" and soaking up the city's unique Stampede spirit.

CHAPTER 2

MUSEUMS

Introduction

In the olden days, museums were rather dull places, with everything shielded by glass and a hushed atmosphere that wasn't particularly inviting to kids. Today, most have interactive stuff, from computer screens featuring videos about rappelling to the chance to climb into, or onto, something intriguing.

Museums such as the Western Heritage Centre in Cochrane welcome families to return again and again. There, little 'uns can pretend to be rodeo cowboys, ranch hands or vets specializing in farm animals. At the Calgary Police Service Interpretive Centre, kids can climb into a cruiser and turn on its lights or use a computer to draw a composite of a crook. Likewise, visitors never get enough of the Olympic Hall of Fame and Museum, with its virtual sports simulators. And if it's art you're after, the Glenbow Museum's galleries, exhibitions and special children's programs generally prove enthralling. Maybe a kids' arts and crafts workshop will be slated for the day of your visit—or perhaps there's storytelling in a teepee. Do a little telephone research before hitting the trail to see what's on the schedule. Other family-friendly museums in this chapter include the Firefighters Museum, the Grain Academy, the Naval Museum of Alberta, the Aero Space Museum and the Museum of the Regiments.

Win Big
OLYMPIC HALL OF FAME AND MUSEUM

88 Canada Olympic Rd. S.W.
Calgary
(403) 247-5452
www.coda.ab.ca/cop

Here's one of the most engaging museums around, with three floors of exhibits and displays of Olympic memorabilia. At the start of your visit, don't miss the rousing Olympic films shown in the theatre. Then, inspect costumes worn by various Olympic participants (with an emphasis on winter sports, since Calgary's Olympic link is to the 1988 Winter Games), medals won and photographs of events.

The museum also has sports simulators. Visitors can pretend to complete a glorious 70-metre ski jump and hurtle down a bobsleigh run. On the third floor, in the interactive Olympic Challenge Gallery,

Seasons and Times

➛ Summer: May 22—Oct 11, daily, 10 am—9 pm (9 am—9 pm, July and August).
Winter: Mid-Nov— mid-March, depending on weather.

Cost

➛ Museum: $7 per person for self-guided tour, $10 per person guided tour, children under 5 free.
Summer and winter C.O.P. season's passes available.

Getting There

➛ By car, take Centre St. north to 16th Ave. Drive west for about 15 kilometres until the Canada Olympic Rd. turnoff (look for the ski jump towers on your left). Free parking on site. About 20 minutes from the Calgary Tower.

➛ By public transit, CT bus 408 offers limited weekday service to the park. Call 262-1000.

➛ By bicycle, C.O.P. is about a 50-minute ride from downtown along City of Calgary trails.

> ☞ **NEARBY**
> ➛ Calaway Park.
>
> ☞ **COMMENT**
> ➛ There are diaper-changing facilities in the larger washrooms. Plan at least a 1-hour visit to the museum.

the whole family can try its hand at various skill-testing aspects of Olympic performance and each member can register his or her efforts in a computer. Children will enjoy climbing the in-house podium to receive a virtual medal.

There are other things to do at Canada Olympic Park, from mountain biking along its trails or attending a kids' ski jump camp in the summer, to whizzing down its slopes on snowboards in the winter. See page 30 for information about the many other activities at the park.

Book'em, Kiddo
THE CALGARY POLICE SERVICE INTERPRETIVE CENTRE

SECOND LEVEL, 316 - 7TH AVE. S.E.
CALGARY
(403) 268-4566
WWW.GOV.CALGARY.AB.CA/POLICE

Real police work is a lot less glamorous than it appears on TV. Fortunately, though, the Calgary Police Service Interpretive Centre doesn't concentrate on tedious paperwork or petty traffic violations. Instead, children will see the kinds of problems police have encountered throughout Calgary's history, from trying to solve crimes using only scant evidence at hand to detecting the difference between real and counterfeit money. Visitors can fingerprint themselves, use a computer and draw a composite of a suspect, sit inside a police car and turn on the flashing lights, dress up in police uniforms and more.

Cleverly arranged, with lots of interactive opportunities, the Centre's frank approach to unveiling the underworld may shock some kids. There are sections on prostitution, domestic violence, drugs, youth gangs and runaways, so be prepared to explain these to your children or avoid the exhibits. Elsewhere, visitors can watch videos about real crimes (appropriate for junior high students and up) and then try solving them.

Young kids should have no real difficulty at the Centre; they won't understand anything you choose not to explain, although sensitive kids may be disturbed by some of

☞ Seasons and Times

➛ Summer: July–Sept, Mon–Thu, 9:30 am–4 pm; weekends, noon–4 pm.
Other times: Mon, 9 am–4 pm; Wed and weekends, noon–4 pm. Staffed by volunteers, so call ahead to confirm the opening hours.

☞ Cost

➛ Adults (18 to 59) $2, children free. An adult must accompany children under 13.

☞ Getting There

➛ Take 9th Ave. east to Macleod Trail. Park underneath the Municipal Building and walk north one block to 7th Ave. then east for a half a block. The Centre is east of the W.R. Castell Public Library. Minutes from the Calgary Tower.

➛ By public transit, take CT bus 10, 9 or 4 and get off at the Municipal building on Macleod Trail at 8th Ave. Cross 7th Ave. and turn east. The Centre is on your left. By LRT, take any downtown train to the City Hall stop. Cross the street and turn east. The museum is on your left.

➛ By bicycle, use the car directions.

the displays. But police work has never been squeaky clean. Educational programs are offered to school groups.

NEARBY

➛ Olympic Plaza, Chinatown, Chinese Canadian Cultural Centre, Glenbow Museum, Arts Centre.

COMMENT

➛ On weekends the elevators don't operate. If your party includes a wheelchair or stroller-user, use the Plus-15 entrance in the Municipal Building to get to the museum, which is on the second floor. Plan at least a 1-hour visit.

All Hands on Deck
NAVAL MUSEUM OF ALBERTA

1820 - 24TH ST. S.W.
CALGARY
(403) 242-0002
WWW.NAVALMUSEUM.AB.CA/

"A navy? In land-locked Alberta?" Parents may marvel, but most children are unlikely to crack wise at the prospect of a museum full of fighter planes, model ships and naval guns. True, not every kid will find this concept appealing, but for those with an active imagination or an interest in military gear, the Naval Museum could be heaven. Visitors can get up close to planes including a Sea Fury F.B. II WG 565, the most powerful fighter ever built, gaze at the downtown skyline through a submarine periscope or listen in on an aerial dogfight in the shadow of a McDonnell F2H Banshee jet fighter.

Uniforms, photos, guns, cannonballs and paintings of ships help tell a tale of adventure and sometimes, tragedy. On the second level, a reproduction of the operational bridge of a Corvette ship gives everyone a glimpse of life on board. Volunteers (mostly veterans) happily show kids around the museum and tell them about Canada's navy, at peace and at war. Videos also explain the museum's contents. There is a movie screen on the premises. Birthday parties can be arranged. The gift shop has naval theme gifts, including clothing and caps.

☞ **Seasons and Times**

➛ July–Aug, daily, 10 am–6 pm. Sept–June, Tue–Fri, 1 pm–5 pm; weekends, 10 am–6 pm. Closed Mondays, excluding holidays.

☞ **Cost**

➛ Adults $5, students and seniors $3, children under 12 $2, families (five or more) $12.
Group rates and memberships available.

☞ **Getting There**

➛ By car, take 9th Ave. east to 1st St. S.E. and drive south to 17th Ave. Turn west on 17th. Proceed to 24th St. and turn south. The museum is on your left. Free parking on site. About 12 minutes from the Calgary Tower.

➛ By public transit, take CT bus 2 (Killarney).

➛ By bicycle, use the car directions.

☞ **Nearby**

➛ Museum of the Regiments.

☞ **Comment**

➛ Plan a 45-minute visit, more if your children are mature or keen on the subject matter.

Making Art at the GLENBOW MUSEUM

130 - 9TH AVE. S.E.
CALGARY
(403) 268-4100
WWW.GLENBOW.ORG

SEASONS AND TIMES

→ Year-round: Daily, 9 am—5 pm. (Thursdays and Fridays open until 9 pm.)
Closed Christmas Day and New Year's.

COST

→ Adults $8, seniors and students $6, youths (6 to 12) $4, under 6 free, families $25 (maximum two adults and four children). Reduced admission Sundays before noon, and Thursdays and Fridays after 5 pm.

GETTING THERE

→ From the Calgary Tower, cross 9th Ave. and walk east. You'll see the Glenbow on your left before you reach the corner.

→ By public transit, take CT bus 10, 9 or 4 and get off the Municipal building on Macleod Trail at 8th Ave. Cross the street, walk west one block, and cross 1st St. S.E. The museum is on your left. By LRT, take the City Centre train and get off at 7th Ave. and 1st St. S.E. Walk south along 1st St. one block. The museum is on your right.

The Glenbow Museum is art central for kids. Before you visit, check out its Web site for a current schedule of activities. Then zero in on the parts of the museum offering kid-friendly activities. Glenbow's Discovery Room is a hands-on area that's an art-maker's paradise, with materials and helpers to assist children in making all kinds of crafts. This inviting spot is sometimes closed, so call ahead.

Some of the museum's permanent exhibitions will appeal to kids. Treasures of the Mineral World features sparkling rocks and light-up displays; Where Symbols Meet, a West African exhibition, has a drum they can try out; and they can admire teepees at the First Nations galleries. Handouts and booklets that make the art more accessible for children are available in some of the galleries.

NEARBY

→ Calgary Tower, Olympic Plaza, Arts Centre, W.R. Castell Library, Calgary Police Interpretive Centre.

COMMENT

→ Plan a 1 to 2-hour visit.

Saturdays (1 to 4 pm) are Family Fun Days at Glenbow, with special presentations for families. Sometimes kids can put on a suit of armor or sit inside a teepee. On certain Saturdays (call for exact dates) the Discovery Cart is rolled out and volunteers present talks and crafts workshops for kids. The museum does not offer birthday parties, but small groups of kids can attend a Family Fun Day or visit the Discovery Room for a relatively cheap birthday activity.

Guided tours are offered to groups with reservations (268-4110).

Food for Thought
THE GRAIN ACADEMY

Plus-15 Level
Roundup Centre, Stampede Park
Calgary
(403) 263-4594

The Grain Academy may not sound like a thrill a minute, but there's more to the place than you imagine. Begin by watching a movie about the olden days on the golden prairie and learn how farmers lived and worked. There's a ceiling-high working model of a country grain elevator and a replica of a 1940s elevator office to inspect. You can run your fingers through different varieties of grain and marvel at their texture, colour and smell. A display of historical farm artifacts helps fill in the blanks on how grain was, and sometimes still is, handled.

The highlight of the visit is seeing the working model of Western Canada's railway grain transportation system. Toy trains chug through a detailed diorama of Rocky Mountain tunnels, passes and valleys on their way to grain terminals in Vancouver. Recorded locomotive sounds lend veracity to the scene.

The museum is suitable for children over six, but younger kids will enjoy watching the trains. Guided tours are probably the best way to explore the Academy, particularly if you're with a group. Schools are welcome; appointments are required. Food isn't easy to come by, so bring snacks and drinks.

☞ Seasons and Times

➛ Year-round: Mon–Fri, 10 am–4 pm; Sat, noon–4 pm (Apr–Sept). Closed all holidays.

☞ Cost

➛ Free. (Donations welcome.)

☞ Getting There

➛ By car, take 9th Ave. east to 1st St. S.E. and turn south. Go east on 12th Ave. to Olympic Way then head south to the park's north entrance. Pay parking on site ($5.50). About seven minutes from the Calgary Tower.

➛ By public transit, take the LRT to Victoria Park Stampede Station. Or take CT bus 10 (Southcentre), which drops you off at the corner of 1st St. and 17th Ave. S.E. Take the pedestrian walkway over to the park.

➛ By bicycle or on foot, use the car directions.

☞ Nearby

➛ Stampede Park, Fort Calgary.

☞ Comment

➛ Plan a 45-minute visit.

Round'em Up
THE WESTERN HERITAGE CENTRE

Hwy. 22
One kilometre north of Cochrane
(403) 932-3514
whcs.ab.ca

Calgary's cowboy heritage extends back over 100 years and Cochrane continues to be a major ranching and rodeo area. The 30-minute drive west to this foothills town is pleasant enough without a visit to the Western Heritage Centre, but the whole family will love it if you make a stop here. The handsome log building with its lovely and big, cozy fireplace holds plenty of appeal. But don't miss the centre's two floors of fascinating information and historic lore about the livestock industry and the sport of rodeo.

The main floor offers movies, tidbits about farm life and interactive displays that allow visitors to get a feel for things such as milking a cow and delivering a calf. Upstairs in the Rodeo Hall of Fame,

Seasons and Times

→ Victoria Day to Thanksgiving, daily, 9 am–5 pm.
Other times: Thu–Sun, 9 am–5 pm.

Cost

→ Adults $7.50, seniors (over 50) and students (12 to 17) $5.50, children (7 to 11) $3.50.
Annual passes and group discounts available.

Getting There

→ By car, take 9th Ave. east to 1st St. S.E. Turn south to 17th Ave. and drive west to Sarcee Trail. Turn north and follow it to the Hwy. 1 turnoff west to Banff and continue until you see the signs for Cochrane. Turn north onto Hwy. 22 and watch for the signs for the Western Heritage Centre turnoff, which is on your right. Free parking on site. About 30 minutes from the Calgary Tower.

☞ **NEARBY**
➛ The trails of Cochrane Ranche Provincial Historic Site.

☞ **COMMENT**
➛ Plan at least a 1-hour visit.

little cowpokes can pretend to ride a horse, drive a chuckwagon or dash through a rodeo chute and rope a calf.

October brings the Cowboy Festival—a weekend full of cowboy poetry, western literature, music and entertainment. Year-round, kids' programs include A Night on the Range with a Western-style supper, ranching activities, a campfire sing-along and more. Reservations are required (932-3659).

The on-site restaurant is fairly pricey so you may prefer to bring a picnic. Explore the trails surrounding the centre until you find a likely lunching place. Or patronize one of the independent establishments in town. For snacking, the Centre's gift shop has old-fashioned stick candy. And every long-time Calgarian knows that Mackay's Cochrane Ice-Cream (220 - 1st St. W., Cochrane 932-2455) is pretty much an obligatory stop.

Atten-shun!! MUSEUM OF THE REGIMENTS

4520 Crowchild Trail S.W.
Calgary
(403) 974-2850

Western Canada's largest military history museum goes a long way toward ensuring future generations remember the sacrifices men and women made in wars. This bunker-like structure is deceivingly dreary-looking from the outside, with its enormous tanks out front. But once you step inside and see the tableaux of soldiers entering a bombed-out area on the basement floor, you understand that these memories have life and breath. The museum is much more than the expected photographs of men in uniform, framed and hung on walls. There are dioramas of famous battles to take in, with taped voices explaining what happened there,

☞ Seasons and Times

→ Year-round: Daily, 10 am–4 pm.

☞ Cost

→ Free. Suggested donations: Adults $5, seniors $3, 12 and under $2.

☞ Getting There

→ By car, take 9th Ave. east to 1st St. S.E. and turn south. Turn west onto 17th Ave. and take the Crowchild south exit. Follow the Flanders Ave. exit west, then turn east at the lights and go over the bridge. Take the first south turn and head west into the parking lot. About 12 minutes from the Calgary Tower.

→ By public transit, take CT buses 7 or 13.

☞ Nearby

→ Naval Museum of Alberta, My Favourite Ice-Cream Shop.

☞ Comment

→ Plan at least a 1-hour visit.

and depictions and descriptions of acts of bravery abound. Children can imagine being brave themselves when they "parachute" out of an aircraft. Elsewhere, there are displays of uniforms and medals, rack upon rack of guns for inspection, plus movies and videos.

Most startling of all is the reproduction of a World War I trench visitors can walk through. It's a dark place lined with sandbags and soldiers and resounding with gunfire. Some children will be spooked by this and might be better off colouring at the tables in the main floor lobby.

The museum offers programs, including a sleep-over that's popular with kids (bring your own foamies and sleeping bags), and there's lots of activity around Remembrance Day when school tours are commonplace. Book well in advance for these services.

Sound the Alarm
FIREFIGHTERS MUSEUM SOCIETY OF CALGARY

4124 - 11TH ST. S.E.
CALGARY
(403) 246-3322

This fairly young facility has a 30-year history—collectors were adding to the society's archives long before it had a building where it could store them. That modest edifice opened in 1999 and now houses all kinds of fascinating artifacts and photos about firefighting, including pictures of "the infernal combustion" truck, the fire department's first motorized vehicle. Young visitors will be impatient to see actual fire trucks and pumps that are housed in a large tent-like structure adjoining the museum. (It's unheated, so bundle up if it's a cool day, or save your visit for warmer weather.) Volunteers (most are retired firefighters) lovingly tend the trucks, including a 1908 horse-drawn pumper. While you can't climb the vehicles, you can "ooh" and "ah" over them to your heart's content.

The best way to enjoy the museum is to arrange for a guided tour. Then children will be able to meet ex-firefighters and ask them questions. This isn't a glitzy museum, but kids with a fondness for trucks and engines will enjoy it.

☞ Seasons and Times

➛ May 1—Thanksgiving, Mon—Sat, 9 am—5 pm; Sun and holidays, noon—5 pm. Other times by appointment.

☞ Cost

➛ Free. Suggested donations: Adults $2, seniors $1. (Part of the proceeds will go toward purchasing pint-size firefighters' uniforms and an interactive computer for kids.)

☞ Getting There

➛ By car, take 9th Ave. east to 1st St. S.E. and turn south (1st St. becomes Macleod Trail). Continue along Macleod until 42nd Ave. and turn east to 11th St. S.E. The museum is on your left. Free parking on site. About 15 minutes from the Calgary Tower.

➛ By public transit, take the Anderson LRT to the 39th Ave. Station transfer to CT bus 30 (Highfield) and ride it to 42nd Ave. and 12th St. S.E. (The bus only operates on weekdays at rush hour.)

☞ Nearby

➛ Stage West.

☞ Comment

➛ The museum has few facilities and no indoor toilets, just two port-a-potties outdoors. Plan a 45-minute visit.

Highflying Fun at the AERO SPACE MUSEUM

4629 McCall Way N.E.
Calgary
(403) 250-3752
www.asmac.ab.ca

Seasons and Times

→ Year-round: Daily, 10 am—5 pm. Closed Christmas Day and New Year's.

Cost

→ Adults $6, seniors and students (12 to 17) $3.50, children (6 to 11) $2, under 6 free, families $15.

Getting There

→ By car, take 9th Ave. to Centre St. and turn north. Turn east onto 16th Ave. and north onto Deerfoot Trail. Take the McKnight Blvd. turnoff. Drive east and turn north onto McCall Way. The museum is on your left. Free parking on site. About 20 minutes from the Calgary Tower.

→ By public transit, take the downtown LRT to the Whitehorn Station and transfer to CT bus 57, which stops across McKnight Blvd. at the Port O'Call Inn Best Western.

Nearby

→ Calgary International Airport.

Comment

→ Picnic tables in the courtyard make lunching here an option when the weather is pleasant. Plan a 45-minute visit.

Less space, more aero-, this museum will appeal most to kids who already delight in lore about flight. That may seem fairly obvious, but the museum features historical memorabilia, archival photographs and a hangar full of planes, both civilian and military, that can only be investigated from the outside. While looking at these static "birds" is interesting, those hoping for something more hands-on may be disappointed. Youngsters can tweak buttons and pull levers in a simulated cockpit. There are also a few tables with crayons and paper where they can draw their own versions of what they see or what they imagine as fine aircraft; however, that's the extent of the interactive quotient.

The museum also puts on tours—most children will appreciate the guidance of an expert. With a minimum of eight kids, a private tour can be arranged (it may include a scavenger hunt) and admission costs less.

CHAPTER 3

IN YOUR NEIGHBOURHOOD

Introduction

You don't have to venture far from home to be entertained. Calgary's neighbourhoods are becoming more and more like villages, with central areas for grocery shopping, watching movies, getting haircuts and buying books. Various service-providers offer diversions for children as a way to forge community bonds.

This chapter takes a look at activities in your neighbourhood, like touring your local fire hall, bowling and doing crafts. All kinds of things are new to kids—even a trip to the farmers' market. A long walk in an off-leash park can provide lots of amusement to a child who is a dog-lover. Watching and identifying the birds gathering at a feeder on a cold winter's afternoon can lead to bird-related reading and art. Getting a haircut can be a real treat when a ride on a mechanical elephant and a short slide into a deep ball room are involved. Swimming pools, skating rinks, bowling alleys, tennis courts and children's libraries are all listed here, as well as some of Calgary's more kid-friendly restaurants.

Places to Paint YOUR OWN POTTERY

Children love painting a plate, a bowl or a mug and then having it fired so it becomes a keepsake. At the following stores, kids are welcome to come in and create a chef d'oeuvre. Prices for smaller objects start at around $10, so it might be a good idea to put a limit on how many pieces they can paint before you get to the store. Projects generally take about 90 minutes, but can take as long as the artist likes. The stores provide the ceramics as well as the brushes and paints, and fires the pottery after the masterpieces are finished. You can pick them up about three days later. Both establisments also host birthday parties.

ART'S DESIRE
1012 - 8TH ST. S.W.
(403) 264-2669

FIRE ESCAPE
1509 - 8TH ST. S.W.
(403) 245-4064

If they like the experience described above, your children might want to participate in a pottery-making workshop. The Parks and Recreation catalogue of pottery (and other) courses for children is available at City of Calgary pools, leisure centres, libraries, as well as large stores and supermarkets. The pottery classes are offered through the arts centres listed below.

CALGARY PARKS AND RECREATION
(403) 268-3888

NORTH MOUNT PLEASANT ARTS CENTRE
523 - 27TH AVE. N.W., CALGARY
(403) 221-3682

WILDFLOWER ARTS CENTRE
3363 SPRUCE DR. S.W., CALGARY
(403) 249-3773

Do It Yourself CRAFTY PLACES

Any dull day can be livened up for a child by learning a new craft. Calgary has all kinds of stores and organizations where staff will teach children how to make anything from teddy bears to hand-painted ceramics to beaded jewellery. A child who likes to collect holiday memorabilia might appreciate a class in making funky scrapbooks. How about hiring someone for your child's next birthday party who can teach the party guests how to make a rain stick out of recycled materials? What about a session of needlepoint instruction for a gaggle of eight-year-olds? Acrylic painting, weaving, making their own glass beads—all these activities expand children's horizons giving them another skill to claim as their own.

SOUTHWEST CALGARY

BEADLES BEADS & DESIGNER JEWELLERY
(CHILDREN'S BIRTHDAY PARTIES AND CLASSES)
1606 - 7TH ST. S.W.
(403) 245-1562

CREATIVE MEMORIES
(403) 278-9670
GLENDA BEARINGER OFFERS CLASSES AND WORKSHOPS (INCLUDING BIRTHDAY PARTIES) FOR CHILDREN AND FAMILIES IN MAKING CREATIVE SCRAPBOOKS AT HER WORKSHOP OR IN YOUR HOME.

IN STITCHES
(NEEDLEWORK AND NEEDLEPOINT CLASSES; BIRTHDAY PARTY WORKSHOPS FOR CHILDREN EIGHT AND UP)
1007 - 11TH AVE. S.W.
(403) 244-4221

LEWISCRAFT
(CRAFTS WORKSHOPS FOR CHILDREN HELD PERIODICALLY)
CHINOOK CENTRE
6455 MACLEOD TRAIL S.
(403) 212-4020

OUT OF HAND
(SEASONAL CLASSES IN TEXTILE-RELATED CRAFTS FOR KIDS SEVEN AND UP; TEDDY BEAR-MAKING CLASSES FOR CHILDREN OVER NINE)
1 - 3919 RICHMOND RD. S.W.
(403) 217-4871

SOAP & MORE THE LEARNING CENTRE
(BIRTHDAY PARTIES, ON THE PREMISES AND IN HOMES, WHERE KIDS FIVE AND UP CAN CREATE BATH BOMBS)
160 WESTWOOD DR. S.W.
(403) 217-2346

SOUTHEAST CALGARY

BEADS & PLENTY MORE
(WORKSHOPS FOR AGES EIGHT AND UP, BIRTHDAY PARTIES FOR KIDS OVER FOUR)
113 - 755 LAKE BONAVISTA DR. S.E.
(403) 278-5056

CAN-AM CERAMIC PRODUCTS
(CERAMIC-PAINTING WORKSHOPS)
4034 - 7TH ST. S.E.
(403) 243-4111

CREATIVE KITS FOR KIDS
(CLASSES AND PARTIES; KITS AND ARTS AND CRAFTS SUPPLIES; CLASSES SPECIALIZING IN PAINTING ON WOOD)
MIDNAPORE VILLAGE, 328 - 22 MIDLAKE BLVD. S.E.
MIDNAPORE
(403) 254-0173

GINA BROWN'S
(CLASSES IN KNITTING AND CROSS-STITCH FOR KIDS 8 TO 12)
BAY 17 6624 CENTRE ST. S.
(403) 255-2200

HANDCRAFTERS COTTAGE
(CLASSES IN PAINTING WITH ACRYLICS ON WOOD FOR KIDS SIX AND UP; SEASONAL THEMES)
DEER VALLEY MALL
1221 CANYON MEADOWS DR. S.E.
(403) 225-1666

SOMETHING SPECIAL
(CREATE-A-CRAFT SESSIONS FOR KIDS FOUR AND UP—CALL AHEAD TO BOOK; BIRTHDAY PARTIES AND BOOKINGS FOR GROUPS)
6622 - 20A ST. S.E.
(403) 279-8888

TANDY LEATHER
(Special classes in working with leather for groups)
180 - 94th Ave. S.E.
(403) 253-3464

NOSTALGIC EXPRESSIONS
(Classes in painting with acrylic on wood for kids five and up; classes for teens; birthday parties)
1213 - 9th Ave. S.E.
(403) 262-8492

Northwest Calgary

CRAFTY KIDS
(Classes for birthdays, Guide and Brownie troupes)
148 Edgedale Dr. N.W.
(403) 239-4677

THE FIBER HUT
(Classes in spinning, off-loom weaving, felting and other textile-related past-times for kids 6 to 12)
2614 - 4th St. N.W.
(403) 230-3822

BEADS & PLENTY MORE
(Workshops for ages eight and up, birthday parties for kids over four)
Northland Village Shoppes, 5111 Northland Dr. N.W.
(403) 288-0153

SCRAPBOOK SALLY
(Card-making, scrapbook-making for groups and birthday parties; classes for ages six and up)
1344 Northmount Dr. N.W.
(403) 210-2244

Northeast Calgary

CREATIVE MEMORIES
(403) 278-9670
Private home in northeast Calgary; call for the address.
Wendy Wallace (293-1258) offers classes and workshops (including birthday parties) in making creative scrapbooks at her workshop or in your home. For families and children age five and up (with a parent).

GREEN'S ROCK & LAPIDARY
(Older children are welcome to attend classes in things lapidary, or to make their own glass beads)
Bay 6 3220 - 5th Ave. N.E.
(403) 571-7625

PMS HOBBY CRAFT
(PAINTING, BEADING AND CAKE DECORATING CLASSES)
2020B 32ND AVE. N.E
(403) 291-2733

PURPLE NEEDLE
(CLASSES IN CROSS-STITCH AND BEADING FOR KIDS EIGHT AND UP; CRAFTS INSTRUCTION AT BIRTHDAY PARTIES)
14 - 222 - 16TH AVE. N.E.
(403) 230-7200

WINSHOP
(CLASSES USING RECYCLED MATERIALS TO MAKE RAIN STICKS AND PAPER; EDUCATIONAL CLASS FOR SCHOOLS)
3811 EDMONTON TR. N.E.
(403) 230-1443

COCHRANE

CRAFT NOOK
(WORKSHOPS FOR KIDS)
312 - 1ST ST.
(403) 932-5944

The Parks and Recreation catalogue of crafts courses for children is available at City of Calgary pools, leisure centres, libraries, as well as large stores and supermarkets. The classes are offered through the Arts Centres listed below.

CALGARY PARKS AND RECREATION
(403) 268-3888

NORTH MOUNT PLEASANT ARTS CENTRE
523 - 27TH AVE. N.W.
(403) 221-3682

WILDFLOWER ARTS CENTRE
3363 SPRUCE DR. S.W.
(403) 249-3773

Rainy-day BOWLING ALLEYS

Is the weather outside frightful? Well then, bowling's so delightful! It lets kids blow off steam, it's reasonably easy and a child's skill set doesn't necessarily depend on his or her height or weight. The whole bowling experience commends it to children—the special shoes, the junk food treats, and the hanging out with family and friends.

Some bowling alleys in Calgary have gilded the lily a bit by offering Glow Bowl, in which the pins glow in the dark, and Bumper Bowling, where the ball can never roll discouragingly into the gutter. Always make sure to call ahead to avoid tournaments and other situations where children aren't welcome. As a birthday party option, bowling may not be trendy (or maybe it is—it's so hard to keep up!) but it's always fun. Ask the staff at your local lanes whether it has birthday packages.

Seasons and Times
➛ Year-round: Daily.

Cost
➛ One game: $2 to $3.
Shoe rental: About $2 a pair.
Birthday packages: Inquire at the alley.

Southwest Calgary

CHINOOK BOWLADROME
Chinook Centre, 6455 Macleod Trail S.
(403) 252- 5747

MOUNTAIN VIEW BOWL
11 - 3919 Richmond Dr. S.W.
(403) 249-0858

Southeast Calgary

BOWLING DEPOT
901 – 64th Ave. N.E.
(403) 275-1260

CALGARY FIVE PIN BOWLERS ASSOCIATION
23B 6020 - 2ND ST. S.E.
(403) 252-5879

CLAYBURN BOWL
1820 - 52ND ST. S.E.
(403) 248- 4664

FRANK SISSON'S SILVER DOLLAR BOWL
1010 - 42ND AVE. S.E.
(403) 287-1183

PARADISE LANES
3411 - 17TH AVE. S.E.
(403) 272-4570

TOPPLER BOWL
7640 FAIRMOUNT DR. S.E.
(403) 255-0101

NORTHWEST CALGARY

FAIRVIEW BOWLING CENTRE
1701 - 16TH AVE. N.W.
(403) 289-2571

THORNCLIFFE GREENVIEW COMMUNITY ASSOCIATION
5600 CENTRE ST. N.
(403) 274-5574

NORTHEAST CALGARY

LET'S BOWL
2916 - 5TH AVE. N.E.
(403) 569-2695

Shopping at a PUBLIC MARKET

There are few excursions quite as pleasurable on a Saturday morning or a summer's evening as a family jaunt to the public market. In Calgary, there's the chance to combine shopping for vegetables with a trip to the petting zoo at the Blackfoot Farmer's Market. Check out the sausages and stroll through the flea market at the Crossroads. Or mesh a trip to the wading pool or a game of catch at Riley Park on a Wednesday afternoon in July or August with a trip across 5th Avenue to the Hillhurst-Sunnyside Farmers' Market. Get up early on a Saturday and leave the city for Millarville, which offers the odd craft (and sometimes craft fair) along with farmers' produce. Give each child a couple of dollars and let them shop along with you, selecting a couple of apples or a loaf of bread to contribute to the family meal.

In wintertime, there's the Eau Claire Market, which, in addition to offering an indoor marketplace featuring bread, fish, meat and produce, provides visitors with a good food fair, entertaining buskers, an IMAX™ theatre and proximity to Prince's Island. An entire day can be pleasantly whiled away in these environs, with a trip to the Eau Claire Y nearby for a family swim or, in summer, a visit to the free splash pool outside the market building.

Please note that the outdoor markets are only open in the summer and fall; call ahead to make sure of hours and times. As of early 2000, Grassroots was considering opening another market elsewhere; call the Grassroots line for more details. Many Calgary-area farms also offer the option of visiting on weekends and purchasing their products. Consult this book's chapter on Animals, Farms and Zoos.

BEARSPAW FARMERS' MARKET

1A HWY. AND NAGWAY RD. N.W.
BEARSPAW
(403) 932-5620

☞ Outdoor farmers' market—slogan is "make it, bake it or grow it." Run by Bearspaw Lions Club; all proceeds go to charity.

☞ First Sunday in June to the 18th Sunday after it. Sun, noon–4 pm.

BLACKFOOT FARMERS' MARKET

5600 - 11TH ST. S.E.
CALGARY
(403) 243-0065

☞ Outdoor market, crafts, petting zoo, playground and park.

☞ June–Oct, Fri–Sat, 8 am–5 pm; Sun, 10 am–4 pm.

CROSSROADS MARKET

2222 - 16TH AVE. N.E.
CALGARY
(403) 291-5208

☞ Indoor farmers' market and flea market.

☞ Year-round: Sat–Sun, 10 am–5 pm. Outdoor market: May–Sept.

EAU CLAIRE MARKET

229 - 200 BARCLAY PARADE S.W.
CALGARY
(403) 264-6460

☞ Indoor market, shops, food fair, movie and IMAX™ theatres.

☞ Year-round: Mon–Wed and Sat, 10 am–6 pm; Thu–Fri, 10 am–9 pm; Sun, 10 am–5 pm (winter: Sun, noon–5 pm).

Grassroots Northland Market
555 - 5111 Northland Dr. N.W.
Calgary
(403) 239-8231

☞ Outdoor farmers' market in Northland Village Mall parking lot.

☞ June 13—Sept 20, Tue, 4 pm—8 pm (rain or shine).

Hillhurst-Sunnyside Farmers' Market
1320 - 5th Ave. N.W.
Calgary
(403) 283-1400

☞ Outdoor farmers' market.

☞ June—Oct, Wed, 3:30 pm—8 pm.

Millarville Farmers' Market
Millarville
(403) 931-2404

☞ Regular outdoor farmers' market and occasional indoor crafts fairs (call or watch local papers for details).

☞ June 10—Sept 30, Sat, 8:30 am—noon.

Visiting Your LOCAL FIRE STATION

(403) 287-4257
www.gov.calgary.ab.ca/fire

Firefighters are proud of what they do and they're happy to show visitors around. Touring a fire station is such a popular activity that the Calgary Fire Department books about 700 groups per year. The size of each group is limited to no more than 30 people. The tour's emphasis is on fire safety and familiarizing children with firefighters and their work. Kids welcome the chance to look at equipment up close and size up the fire trucks. They even receive a colouring book at the end of their visit. The tour is restricted to children over the age of four.

> **☞ Seasons and Times**
> ➛ Tours are conducted three times a day, seven days a week but must be booked at least seven days in advance.
>
> **☞ Cost**
> ➛ Free.
>
> **☞ Comment**
> ➛ Groups must include at least one adult for every five children. The tours last 30 to 45 minutes, depending on the number of questions the kids lob at the firefighters.

Cruising to Your LOCAL POLICE STATION

Because Calgary City Police like to be accessible to everyone in the community, including kids, they welcome tours for groups of up to 20 people at some district offices. Kids can troop through the parade rooms (where officers gather and start each shift), team offices, interview rooms, detective offices and the garage, where the police cars are parked. Some districts have more to see than others do—a much more comprehensive view of police work can be gained at the Calgary Police Service Interpretive Centre (page 40). More frequently, the department sends officers out to talk to groups of any age, including Scouts, Guides and kindergartens, on a range of subjects, from bullying to protecting yourself from crime. According to one such officer, no group is too small to get this kind of attention from their local unit. Kids get to check out the squad car, sound the siren and do other neat stuff.

To arrange a tour or a visit, call the Community Liaison officer in your area. You'll find the listing in the City of Calgary blue pages in your local phone book.

Dining Out at KID-FRIENDLY RESTAURANTS

Going out for a meal with the family can be a real treat or a real trauma, depending on how you're received. While taking your toddlers to dine at La Chaumiere or Concorde isn't likely to win you any fans with the wait staff, kids are welcomed with warm smiles at many of the city's more moderately-priced restaurants. In this situation it's always a good idea to take a colouring book and a few markers with you, and the wise parent usually has a packet of soda crackers or two in case there's a wait for service. But family-friendly restaurants are likely to provide crayons and menus children can colour, food aimed at their conservative tastes, and sometimes even a little toy at the end of the outing. That kind of treatment keeps families going back for more. Before heading out with the gang, call ahead and ask if the restaurant has high chairs or booster seats.

CAFÉ METRO
(INTERESTING DECOR; DELI FOOD)
17 - 7400 MACLEOD TRAIL S. • (403) 255-6537

THE CEDARS DELI & RESTAURANT
(LEBANESE FOOD; PLEASANT, INFORMAL ATMOSPHERE)
1009A 1ST ST. S.W. • (403) 264-2532
EAU CLAIRE MARKET • (403) 263-5232
225 - 8TH AVE. S.W. • (403) 263-0285

COMMUNITY NATURAL FOODS
(CAFETERIA-STYLE VEGETARIAN DINING; WHOLESOME FOOD)
1304 -10TH AVE. S.W. • (403) 229-2383

EARL'S
(PASTAS, PIZZAS AND OTHER KID-PLEASING FOODS; FRIENDLY STAFF; BEST FOR OLDER KIDS; THE EARL'S CHAIN HAS OTHER LOCATIONS AS WELL AS THOSE LISTED BELOW)
1110 16TH AVE. N.W. • (403) 289-2566
2401 4TH ST. S.W. • (403) 228-4141
3030 23RD ST. N.E. • (403) 291-6700
3012 17TH AVE. S.E. • (403) 273-3275

4 STREET ROSE RESTAURANT & BAR
(OLDER CHILDREN WILL APPRECIATE THE TRENDY, KID-FRIENDLY FOOD AND INFORMAL ATMOSPHERE)
2116 - 4TH ST. S.W. • (403) 245-1888

HEARTLAND CAFÉ
(HEALTHY MENU; MUFFINS, SOUPS, SALADS)
940 - 2ND AVE. N.W. • (403) 270-4541

JACK ASTOR'S BAR & GRILL
(KIDS' MENU; FRIENDLY WAITERS; KID-SIZE DESSERTS)
9823 MACLEOD TRAIL S. • (403) 252-2246
5909 SIGNAL HILL COURT • (403) 249-4300

JOEY TOMATO'S KITCHEN
(PIZZA, PASTA, LOUD AND FRIENDLY ATMOSPHERE; BETTER FOR OLDER KIDS)
10456 SOUTHPORT RD. S.W. • (403) 271-3575
208 BARCLAY PARADE S.W. • (403) 263-6336

KELSEY'S RESTAURANT
(KIDS' MENU; CRAYONS AND COLOURING SHEETS; TOYS)
EAU CLAIRE MARKET • (403) 269-5599
900 - 3545 - 32NDAVE. N.E. • (403) 291-3145
415 - 5005 DALHOUSIE DR. N.W. (403) 286-0990
5620 SIGNAL HILL COURT • (403) 217-7780

Little Vietnamese Village Restaurant
(great, fresh Vietnamese noodles and other staples in Chinatown)
138 - 3rd Ave. S.E. • (403) 266-4114

Montana's Restaurant
(kids' menu; cowboy cuisine; Western paraphernalia; toys)
5562 Signal Hill Court • (403) 217-1100
112 Crowfoot Terrace N.W. • (403) 241-9740

The Old Spaghetti Factory
(kids' menu; pasta; better for older kids)
222 - 3rd St. S.W. • (403) 263-7223

Outwest
(kids' menu; family dining on cowboy cuisine)
Eau Claire Market • (403) 262-9738

Red Lobster
(kids' menu, crayons, toys)
312 - 35th St. N.E. • (403) 248-8111
100 - 6100 Macleod Trail S.W. • (403) 252-8818
2316 - 16th Ave. N.W. • (403) 282-0952

Red Robin Restaurant
(kids' menus, crayons, colouring sheet)
101 - 10th St. N.W. • (403) 283-9600
Bldg. E, 9727 Macleod Trail S. • (403) 259-3915
3575 – 20th Ave. N.E. • (403) 293-4047

Royal Seoul Restaurant
(Korean fare; casual atmosphere)
1324 - 10th Ave. S.W. • (403) 228-1120

Sante Fe Grill
(kids' menu, crayons, colouring sheet)
9250 Macleod Trail S.W. • (403) 253-9096
322 - 11th Ave. S.W. • (403) 262-7262

Santorini Greek Taverna
(classic Greek fare)
1502 Centre St. N. • (403) 276-8363

Spiros Pizza
(good pizza and Greek food, toys)
1902 - 33rd St. S.W.
(403) 242-04443

Sushi Hiro Japanese Restaurant
(sushi and other Japanese foods; tatami rooms)
727 - 5th Ave. S.W.
(403) 233-0605

SUSHI SHINO
(SUSHI AND OTHER JAPANESE FOODS IN THE HEART OF CHINATOWN)
DRAGON CITY MALL
128 - 328 CENTRE ST. S.
(403) 262-8805

Buffets are popular with children because they allow kids to choose exactly what they want, in the perfect proportions.

MOTI MAHAL
(INDIAN BUFFET; CAN BE SPICY)
201 - 1805 - 14TH ST. S.W. • (403) 228-9990

PALLISER OAK ROOM
(SPECIAL OCCASION SUNDAY BRUNCH; PRICEY)
133 – 9TH AVE. S.W. • (403) 262-1234

REGENCY PALACE
(CHINESE BUFFET; ICE CREAM FOR DESSERT; FISH POND)
328 CENTRE ST. S.E. • (403) 777-2288

PANORAMA REVOLVING RESTAURANT
(CALGARY TOWER)
(WEEKEND BRUNCHES WITH A BREATHTAKING VIEW)
101 - 9TH AVE. S.W. • (403) 266-7171

TAJ MAHAL RESTAURANT
(DAILY VEGETARIAN LUNCH BUFFET)
4816 MACLEOD TRAIL S. • (403) 243-6362

These popular fast food establishments have restaurants all over Calgary. Why not make it a kids' night out and stroll to the outlet nearest you?

ARBY'S
BURGER KING
HARVEY'S
KFC
MCDONALD'S
SUBWAY
SWISS CHALET
TACO BELL
TIM HORTON'S DONUTS
ROBIN'S DONUTS
WENDY'S

Combing the Area for CHILDREN'S HAIRCUTTERS

There's no need for a haircut to be a traumatic event. Certain hair salons now cater to kids so well that they'll beg for "just a little off the sides"—even when they don't need it. While at the salon kids can watch videos and sit on an animal-shaped ride. They can even request sparkle gel in their hair. While they're waiting for their turn, they can jump around in a ball room specifically installed for restless clients. The great thing is, these haircuts are good, they aren't super-pricey, and everyone emerges from the experience smiling. Birthday parties in such establishments offer groups of girls the fun of temporary streaks of hair-colour, braiding and styling, and makeup and nail polish sessions.

BEANERS FUN CUTS FOR KIDS
3408 BOW TRAIL S.W. • (403) 217-1444
311 - 4820 NORTHLAND DR. N.W. • (403) 220-1444
8330 MACLEOD TRAIL S. • (403) 255-2774

KIDS PLAY FUN HAIR DESIGNS
8 - 250 CROWFOOT COURT. N.W. • (403) 241-5537
22 - 7337 SIERRA MORENA BLVD. S.W. • (403) 217-901

Read All about It CHILDREN'S LIBRARIES

HTTP://PUBLIC-LIBRARY.CALGARY.AB.CA

Every one of Calgary's public libraries has a children's section, and each one also offers free programs for kids. Storytelling sessions, which are geared to particular age groups, are a terrific way to entertain a child and his or her friends. Pick up a brochure detailing programs at the library in your neighbourhood, and make sure to find out whether you need to book ahead for the ones that interest your family. You can also look up programs on the Calgary Public Library Web site (above), clicking first on Library Services, then on Library Locations, and then on the location that interests you.

SOUTHWEST CALGARY

ALEXANDER CALHOUN LIBRARY
3223 - 14TH ST. S.W.
(403) 221-2010

MEMORIAL PARK LIBRARY
1221 - 2ND ST. S.W.
(403) 221-2006

SHAGANAPPI LIBRARY
3415 - 8TH AVE. S.W.
(403) 221-2020

SIGNAL HILL LIBRARY
5994 SIGNAL HILL COURT S.W.
(403) 221-2000

SOUTHWOOD LIBRARY
924 SOUTHLAND DR. S.W.
(403) 221-2082

SOUTHEAST CALGARY

FISH CREEK AREA LIBRARY
11161 BONAVENTURE DR. S.E.
(403) 221-2090

FOREST LAWN LIBRARY
4807 - 8TH AVE. S.E.
(403) 221-2070

MIDNAPORE LIBRARY
MIDNAPORE MALL
2 - 240 MIDPARK WAY S.E.
(403) 221-2072

MILLICAN-OGDEN LIBRARY
7005 - 18TH ST. S.E.
(403) 221-2080

NORTHWEST CALGARY

BOWNESS LIBRARY
7930 BOWNESS RD. N.W.
(403) 221-2022

GEORGINA THOMSON LIBRARY
51 CORNELL RD. N.W.
(403) 221-2040

LOUISE RILEY LIBRARY
1904 - 14TH AVE. N.W.
(403) 221-2046

NOSE HILL LIBRARY
1530 NORTHMOUNT DR. N.W.
(403) 221-2030

NORTHEAST CALGARY

THORN-HILL LIBRARY
6617 CENTRE ST. N.
(403) 221-2050

VILLAGE SQUARE LIBRARY
2623 - 56TH ST. N.E.
(403) 221-2060

Towns near Calgary

ACME

ACME SCHOOL LIBRARY
601 WALSH AVE.
(403) 546-3845

AIRDRIE

AIRDRIE PUBLIC LIBRARY
704 MAIN ST. S.
(403) 948-0600

BEISEKER

MUNICIPAL LIBRARY
700 - 1ST AVE.
(403) 947-3230

CARSTAIRS

BOB CLARK MUNICIPAL LIBRARY
1135 OSLER ST.
(403) 337-3943

COCHRANE

NAN BOOTH MEMORIAL LIBRARY
213 - 1ST AVE. W.
(403) 932-4353

CREMONA

CREMONA MUNICIPAL LIBRARY
205 - 1ST ST. E.
(403) 637-3762

CROSSFIELD

CROSSFIELD MUNICIPAL LIBRARY
1026 CHISHOLM AVE.
(403) 946-4232

HIGH RIVER

CENTENNIAL LIBRARY
909 1ST ST. W.
(403) 652-2917

IRRICANA

IRRICANA & DISTRICT MUNICIPAL LIBRARY
IRRICANA SPORTS COMPLEX
(403) 935-4818

OKOTOKS

OKOTOKS PUBLIC LIBRARY
7 RIVERSIDE DR.
(403) 938-2220

BLACK DIAMOND/ TURNER VALLEY

SHEEP RIVER PUBLIC LIBRARY
301 CENTRE AVE.
(403) 933-3278

STRATHMORE

STRATHMORE MUNICIPAL LIBRARY
85 LAKESIDE BLVD.
(403) 934-5440

Cool Places to Play
SWIMMING POOLS

Swimming pools have come a long way since the ol' swimmin' hole of days gone by. Programming at public pools now includes movie nights and kayaking lessons, Halloween bashes, children's birthday and teen pool parties, synchronized swimming instruction and lessons for parents and tots. Don't forget the leisure centres too, where one child can be skating with friends while his or her siblings are racing down waterslides in the pool area. Here's a listing of Calgary's indoor and outdoor pools. For City of Calgary pool schedules, call the Playline at (403) 268-2300 and enter the code of the pool, as listed below. The asterisks denote the salt-water pools; easier on the skin and eyes than the chlorinated ones.

Indoor Pools

SOUTHWEST CALGARY

BELTLINE POOL & FITNESS CENTRE
223 - 12TH AVE. S.W. • CODE 9820

CANYON MEADOWS POOL
& FITNESS CENTRE *
89 CANOVA RD. S.W. • CODE 9840

EAU CLAIRE YMCA
101 - 3RD ST. S.W.
(403) 269-6701

COMMUNITY/INTERNATIONAL
YMCA
620 - 604 - 1ST ST. S.W.
(403) 531-1660

GLENMORE POOL *
5330 - 19TH ST. S.W. • CODE 9860

KILLARNEY POOL
17TH AVE. AND 29TH ST. S.W.
CODE 9870

LINDSAY PARK SPORTS CENTRE
2225 MACLEOD TRAIL S.
(403) 233-8393

ROCKY MOUNTAIN YMCA
225 - 604 - 1ST ST. S.W.
(403) 269-6156

SOUTHLAND LEISURE CENTRE
2000 SOUTHLAND DR. S.W.
(403) 251-3505

SOUTH YMCA
11 HADDON RD. S.W.
(403) 255-8131

Southeast Calgary

ACADIA POOL & FITNESS CENTRE*
9009 Fairmount Dr. S.E. • Code 9810

BOB BAHAN POOL & FITNESS CENTRE *
4812 - 14th Ave. S.E. • Code 9830

INGLEWOOD POOL *
1527 - 17th Ave. S.E. • Code 9760

YWCA OF CALGARY
320 - 5th Ave. S.E. • (403) 263-1550

Northwest Calgary

CROWFOOT YMCA
8100 John Laurei Blvd. N.W.
(403) 547-6576

FOOTHILLS POOL
2915 - 24th Ave. N.W. • Code 9840

SHOULDICE POOL *
5303 Bowness Rd. N.W. • Code 9740

SIR WINSTON CHURCHILL POOL & FITNESS CENTRE *
1520 Northmount Dr. N.W.
Code 9730

THORNHILL POOL & FITNESS CENTRE
6725 Centre St. N.W. • Code 9750

Northeast Calgary

BISHOP MCNALLY YMCA
5700 Falconridge Blvd. N.E.
(403) 285-7444

RENFREW POOL & FITNESS CENTRE *
810 - 13th Ave. N.E. • Code 9880

VILLAGE SQUARE LEISURE CENTRE
2623 - 56th St. N.E.
(403) 280-9714

Towns near Calgary

Acme

ACME SWIMMING POOL
219 Alison St. • (403) 546-3017

Airdrie

EAST LAKE AQUA CENTRE
800 East Lake Blvd. • (403) 948-8804

Cochrane

BIGHILL LEISURE POOL
201 - 5th Ave. • (403) 932-2674

High River

BOB SNODGRASS RECPLEX
129 - 3rd Ave. S.W. • (403) 652-4041

Okotoks

OKOTOKS SWINDELLS POOL
OKOTOKS RECREATION CENTRE
99 Okotoks Dr. • (403) 938-5094

Outdoor Pools

Open mid-June to Labour Day. Asterisks denote the salt-water pools. For further information on outdoor pools, call: the Playline at (403) 268-2300, code 9600.

Northwest Calgary

Bowview
1910 - 6th Ave. N.W.

Highwood
25 Holmwood Ave. N.W.

Mount Pleasant
2310 - 6th St. N.W.

Silver Springs
Silverridge Dr.
and Silverridge Cl. N.W.

Northeast Calgary

Bridgeland *
919 McDougall Rd. N.E.

Southeast Calgary

Forest Lawn
1706 - 39th St. S.E.

Millican
69th Ave. and 20A St. S.E.

Southwest Calgary

South Calgary *
3130 - 16th St. S.W.

Stanley Park
4011 - 1A St. S.W.

Other towns

Strathmore

Strathmore Swimming Pool
170 Brent Blvd. • (403) 934-3325

Wading Pools

Open mid-June through Labour Day. For further information on wading pools, call the Playline at: (403) 268-2300, code 9600.

Southwest Calgary

Barclay Mall Wading & Spray Pool
1st Ave. and 3rd St. S.W.

Stanley Park Wading Pool
4011 - 1A St. S.W.

Northwest Calgary

Bowness Park Spray Pool
8900 - 48th Ave. N.W.

Canmore Park Wading Pool
9th St. and Chicoutimi Dr. N.W.

Highwood Pool
25 Holmwood Ave. N.W.

Mount Pleasant Wading Pool
2310 - 6th St. N.W.

Riley Park Wading Pool
800 - 12th St. N.W.

Northeast Calgary

Prairie Winds Park Wading & Spray Pool
223 Castleridge Blvd. N.E.

Rotary Park Wading Pool
617 - 1st St. N.E. • (403) 276-3203

Cool Places to Play II
CITY RINKS

If you live in the Northern Hemisphere, learning to skate is pretty much obligatory. Falling in love with skating seems to follow. There's no dearth of places in Calgary to strap on the blades and glide along. A spectacular venue is the lagoon at Bowness Park, where a moonlight skate is always enticing. There's also the Olympic Oval (page 83), an immense indoor rink built for the best speed skaters Canada has to offer. When it's minus-whatever and you can't face the local outdoor rinks, the Oval is a comfortable alternative. For lesson times and hockey schedules, call the Playline at 268-2300, code 9350. To make a booking for ice times, arena rentals or tournaments, call (403) 268-3850. Get out there and carve up some ice!

SOUTHWEST CALGARY

OPTIMIST/GEORGE BLUNDUN
5020 - 26TH AVE. S.W.

ROSE KOHN/JIMMIE CONDON
502 HERITAGE DR. S.W.

SOUTHLAND LEISURE CENTRE/
A & B (JUSTICE JOSEPH KRYCZKA)
2000 SOUTHLAND DR. S.W.

STU PEPPARD (GLENMORE)
5300 - 19TH ST. S.W.

SOUTHEAST CALGARY

ERNIE STARR
4804 - 14TH AVE. S.E.

FRANK McCOOL
1900 LAKE BONAVISTA DR. S.E.

NORTHWEST CALGARY

FATHER DAVID BAUER/
NORMA BUSH
2424 UNIVERSITY DR. N.W.

SHOULDICE
1515 HOME RD. N.W.

NORTHEAST CALGARY

HENRY VINEY/STEW HENDRY
814 - 13TH AVE. N.E.

MURRAY COPOT THORNHILL
6715 CENTRE ST. N.

VILLAGE SQUARE LEISURE
CENTRE 1 & 2
2623 - 56TH ST. N.E.

Towns near Calgary

ACME
ACME (OUTDOOR) SKATING RINK
117 ALISON ST. • (403) 546-3783

AIRDRIE
PLAINSMEN ARENA
320 CENTRE AVE. E. • (403) 948-5759

AIRDRIE AND DISTRICT REC COMPLEX
(TWIN ARENAS)
200 EAST LAKE CRES. • (403) 948-4242

BEISEKER
BEISEKER ARENA
410 - 5TH ST. • (403) 947-3855

CARSTAIRS
CARSTAIRS MEMORIAL ARENA
END OF HAMMOND ST.
(403) 337-3391

CROSSFIELD
PETE KNIGHT MEMORIAL ARENA
920 MOUNTAIN AVE. • (403) 946-5822

HIGH RIVER
BOB SNODGRASS RECPLEX
129 - 3RD AVE. S.W. • (403) 652-4041

OKOTOKS
MURRAY ARENA
PIPER ARENA
OKOTOKS RECREATION CENTRE
99 OKOTOKS DR. • (403) 938-5094

SPRINGBANK
SPRINGBANK PARK FOR ALL SEASONS
181ST AND SPRINGBANK RD. S.W.
(403) 242-2223

STRATHMORE
STRATHMORE FAMILY CENTRE (ARENA)
160 BRENT BLVD. • (403) 934-2996

Rallying at PUBLIC TENNIS COURTS

Tennis: a great sport, a wonderful way to soak up the summer sun, and terrific exercise. Why not get the whole family involved? Whether you're practicing, fooling around or really engaged in serious court combat, a good time will be had by all. The City of Calgary and its various communities own and operate numerous public tennis courts at 95 sites scattered throughout the city.

Private clubs sometimes let the public in if they book the same day they play. And tennis lessons are available through the courts themselves and through local sports shops.

City of Calgary and Community Courts

(403) 268-3888

On city-owned courts during prime time, players pay $4 per hour, per court. During non-prime time hours, the nets automatically come up and players can play for free. Prime time hours are: Monday to Friday, 11 am to 2 pm and 5 pm to 8 pm; Saturdays, Sundays and holidays, 9 am to 8:30 pm. (Make sure night lights are in service before dropping children off at night at a city tennis court.) On all city courts, there is a time limit of one hour if people are waiting to play. For information on tennis lessons on city courts, call Tennis Associates at (403) 202-4798. There are no city-owned indoor tennis courts.

Calgary Racquet & Athletic Club

2121 - 98th Ave. S.W.
(403) 281-4481
Non-members are allowed to play if they book a court for the same day. Members can book ahead.

Rico Tennis Academy

19th St. and 56th Ave. S.W.
(403) 243-6717
Indoor courts.

Shaw-nee Slopes Golf Course

820 – 146th Ave. S.W.
(403) 256-6224
Outdoor courts without cover.

Chapter 4

Places to Play

Introduction

Kids: no matter what the season, they're eager to play, set for adventure, raring to go. Fortunately for them, Calgary is filled with destinations where family fun is the number-one priority. This chapter tells you all you'll need to know about the sites so you can be as ready as your children are. When the weather turns nasty, head indoors and spend the day at one of Calgary's wave pools, where the surf's up year-round. There's no shortage of indoor playgrounds for exploring, or take refuge at a McDonald's™ or Burger King™ play area. When the sun is shining, round up the gang and head to the beach or a spray pool. Thrill-seekers will get a rush from whitewater rafting. Or head to Wintergreen Golf and Ski Resort, the ideal destination for families who like being outdoors whatever the season. This chapter will also tell you where to find indoor rock climbing, go-carting, laser tag and capture the flag, as well as the locations of the city's best tobogganing hills.

Choose your destination, then get cracking. And be prepared for lots of smiles.

Breaking Records at THE OLYMPIC OVAL

2500 UNIVERSITY DR. N.W.
CALGARY
(403) 220-7890

Built for the 1988 XV Winter Olympic Games, the Olympic Oval boasts the "fastest ice in the world": most official world records in long track speed skating have been set here. While the Oval continues to be a popular venue for competitions, your kids can streak around the 400 metres of beautifully maintained ice during public skating hours. Skating aids and helmets are at hand for youngsters just learning to balance on their blades and both hockey and speed skates can be rented (speed skates are not available in the smallest sizes). Two international-size ice arenas and a 450-metre running track complete the facility.

The Olympic Oval hosts a number of special events throughout the year, including Family Fun Days, a Halloween

☞ SEASONS AND TIMES

→ Year-round: Daily. Call for public skating times. Closed during competitions.

☞ COST

→ Skating: Adults $4, seniors, youths and children $2, 5 and under free, families $9.
Rentals: Hockey skates $3.50, speed skates $3.75, helmets and skating aids free (deposit of ID required). Credit cards accepted for transactions over $5.

☞ GETTING THERE

→ By car, take Centre St. north to 6th Ave. S.W. (its name changes to Bow Trail) and go west. Turn north on Crowchild Trail, then west on University Dr. N.W. At 24th Ave. N.W. turn west and continue to Collegiate Rd. Parking is available in either Lot 10 ($1.50) or Lot 11 ($2.25). About 15 minutes from the Calgary Tower.
→ By public transit, take CT bus 9.

☞ NEARBY

→ University of Calgary Outdoor Program Centre Climbing Wall.

party and a Christmas party. During these events, the entertainment may include tobogganing (snow is brought into the building), sleigh rides, singers, performers, plus figure skating and freestyle skiing demonstrations.

Play All Day at SOUTHLAND LEISURE CENTRE

2000 Southland Park Dr. S.W.
Calgary
(403) 251-3505

Southland Leisure Centre offers something for everyone in the family. While older children shoot baskets or enjoy a game of badminton in the gym, energetic tots can explore the pint-size ball-crawl, tunnels and castles in the Kinderroom. Tumblers of all ages will be delighted with the gymnastics room, where a certified supervisor will give

> **Seasons and Times**
> ➛ Year-round: Daily. Call the centre for a complete schedule of activities.
>
> **Cost**
> ➛ Adults $7.75, seniors and children (7 to 17) $4.25, preschoolers (2 to 6) $2, under 2 free, families $17.
> Skating: Adults $3.75, seniors and children (7 to 17) $2, preschoolers (2 to 6) $1, under 2 free, families $8.25.
> Discounted admission 45 minutes to one hour before closing every day and on Tuesdays after 7 pm. Ten-pass cards and annual passes available. Credit cards accepted.

tips on tackling everything from the trampoline to the beam and bars. The centre also has a climbing wall that's supervised and offers year-round ice-skating.

With your children happily occupied, you might just have time to take in a fitness class of your own. But whatever you decide to do, don't leave without visiting the wave pool. Rope swings, a diving tank and two large waterslides will occupy older children and adults; a smaller tunnel slide and warm-water wading pool with a kiddie-size slide and a colourful array of water-spouts are for youngsters.

Birthday party packages and childcare are offered. Call the centre for information about its recreational programs and swimming classes.

☞ **Getting There**

➛ By car, take 9th Ave. east to 1st St. S.E. (its name changes to Macleod Trail) and go south. Turn west on Southland Dr. and continue to 19th St. S.W. Turn right into the parking lot. Free parking on site. About 25 minutes from the Calgary Tower.

➛ By public transit, take the south-bound (Anderson) LRT to Southland Station and transfer to CT bus 56.

☞ **Similar Attraction**

➛ **Village Square Leisure Centre,** 2623 - 56th St. N.E., Calgary (403) 280-9714.

Get Moving at THE FAMILY LEISURE CENTRE

11150 Bonaventure Dr. S.E.
Calgary
(403) 278-7542

Whether you enjoy racquetball or squash, skating or curling, the Family Leisure Centre has something for you. There's also a gym, a weight room, a dance room and two arts and crafts studios, but the biggest attraction by far is the wave pool, where a heart-pounding 96-metre water slide, a rope swing and a volleyball net await your kids.

When the surf's up, older children will love romping in the breakers at the wave pool. A gentle slope into the pool lets toddlers and younger children join in the fun. Or steer them to the shallow play area, located in a quiet corner of the main pool, with its kiddie-size slide. When everyone's beginning to droop, the centre's hot tub and steam rooms provide a relaxing break.

Qualified lifeguards staff the centre, and there is swimming instruction as well as recreational

Seasons and Times

➛ Year-round: Daily. Call the centre for a complete schedule of activities.

Cost

➛ Adults $7.25, seniors $5, children (6 to 17) $4, preschoolers (2 to 5) $1.75, under 2 free, families $16.30.
Skating: Adults $4, seniors $2, children (6 to 17) $2.25, preschoolers (2 to 5) $1, under 2 free, families $9.
Squash/racquetball: $9 for 45 minutes (prime time), $7 for 45 minutes (non-prime time).
Discounted admission: Mon—Thu, 6 am—4 pm; Fri, 6 am—1 pm; Mon—Thu and Sun, 7 pm—closing. Ten-pass cards and annual passes available. Credit cards accepted.

programs for all levels. Birthday party packages and childcare are available.

Getting There

→ By car, take 9th Ave. east to 1st St. S.E. (its name changes to Macleod Trail) and go south. Turn east on Willow Park Dr., then south on Bonaventure Dr. The Family Leisure Centre is on your left. Free parking on site. About 25 minutes from the Calgary Tower.

→ By public transit, take CT bus 10 to the west side of the Family Leisure Centre.

Similar Attraction

→ **Village Square Leisure Centre,** 2623 – 56th St. N.E., Calgary (403) 280-9714.

Great Places to Get Wet
SPRAY POOLS

Run through a tunnel of water, stand beneath a cooling spray, block a fountain with your toes. On a hot day, a spray pool can be paradise. Although older children will be happy getting as wet as they can, some toddlers may object to all the splashing. At most sites, grassy spots and benches provide a perfect spot for parents to set up base. Toilets, playgrounds, picnic tables and concession stands are usually found nearby.

Bowness Park
8900 – 48th Ave. N.W., Calgary

Eau Claire Market (Barclay Parade)
Off Barclay Parade, S.W., Calgary

Prairie Winds Park
Off Castleridge Blvd. N.E., Calgary

Scheming and Strategizing CAPTURE THE FLAG & PAINTBALL ADVENTURE

1912 Mackay Rd. N.W.
Calgary
(403) 247-8887
www.capturetheflag.com

Combine a fast-paced game of tag with a stealthy game of hide-and-seek and you've got paintball. Although game variations exist, the general aim is to capture the other team's flag while protecting your own. At the same time, each contingent tries to tag, with a paintball, players from the opposing side.

Capture the Flag & Paintball Adventure has two locations and welcomes children ten and up to play either indoors, amidst 15,000 square metres of buildings, bunkers and barricades, or outdoors in a 44-hectare wilderness area. Outdoors, 12 separate courses offer endless opportunities for adventure. Prowl around a 1.2-hectare urban wipeout

☞ Seasons and Times

➛ Outdoor game field: Year-round, daily during daylight hours. Reservations are recommended, although walk-on players are welcome after 1 pm.
Indoor arena: Year-round, daily, 10 am–10 pm. Reservations are recommended. After-hours access is available on request.

☞ Cost

➛ Outdoor game field: $6.50 per person per day (includes equipment rental, selected beverages, hot dogs, camping, and barbecue and bunkhouse access). $20 for 125 paintballs.
Indoor arena: $6.50 per person per 1-hour session (includes equipment rental). $8 for 50 paintballs.
Group specials available. Credit cards accepted.

scene that's complete with parked cars and buses or try the 16-hectare wooded site. For those with little-to-no directional sense, the courses are fenced and studded with maps. A rumpus room with fireplace is a place to warm up on colder days.

The indoor location features a somewhat decrepit and smoky birthday party room and spectator gallery (also a licensed lounge). Laser tag is available for kids five and up.

☞ Getting There

Outdoor game field:

➛ By car, take Centre St. north to 6th Ave. S.W. (its name changes to Bow Trail) and drive west. Turn north on Sarcee Trail, then west on the Trans-Canada Hwy. Follow it to Hwy. 22 and head north to Cochrane. Once through the town of Cochrane, turn west onto Hwy. 1A and continue on for 13 kilometres. Turn north onto the 940 Secondary Rd. (Old Forestry Trunk Rd.), drive for 22 kilometres and follow the Kruger Capture the Flag signs to the site. Free parking on site. About one hour from the Calgary Tower.

Indoor arena:

➛ By car, take Centre St. north to 6th Ave. S.W. (its name changes to Bow Trail) and go west. Turn north on Crowchild Trail, then west again on Memorial Dr. (its name changes once to Parkdale Blvd. and again to Bowness Rd.). Turn right on 42nd St. N.W. and follow the road to the junction of 19th Ave. and Mackay Rd. N.W. Free parking on site. About 15 minutes from the Calgary Tower.

➛ By public transit, take CT bus 1.

☞ Comment

➛ The vegetable oil paint is water soluble and washes easily out of both clothing and hair. A paintball shot can sting, however, the full-face safety gear (supplied) protects the face, and overalls and camouflage gear (supplied) will absorb some of the impact.

☞ Similar Attraction

➛ **Paintball Zone,** 1640 - 17A St. S.E., Calgary (403) 282-0827.

High-tech Hide-and-seek LASER TAG

Add black lights, swirling fog and a bit of hi-tech wizardry to a game of hide-and-seek and you've got the perfect recipe for fun. Players travel through a darkened multi-level maze while using laser guns to "tag" their opponents and score points electronically. High scorers can earn a different "firearm"—sometimes a rapid-fire weapon—and some facilities offer stationary targets, which are a bonus for younger children. To ensure everyone has fun, a marshal keeps an eye on the action. After the game, players can obtain a computer analysis that will give them their ranking. Birthday parties can be arranged at all locations.

Kart Gardens/Kart World Family Fun Centre

5202 - 1ST ST. S.W.
CALGARY
(403) 253-8301

At just over 1,800 square metres, this smaller maze suits individual groups wishing to play by themselves. Kart Gardens/Kart World also offers video games, go-carting, minigolf and bumper boats.

☞ **SEASONS AND TIMES**

➛ Apr 1—Oct 31, daily, 11 am—10 pm (hours may be reduced in the spring and fall). Reservations required.

☞ **COST**

➛ $4 per 7.5-minute game or $7 per 15-minute game. Credit cards accepted.

Laser Quest

9827 HORTON RD. S.W.
CALGARY
(403) 640-1245
WWW.LASERQUEST.COM

Over 11,000 square metres of fun for kids seven and up. Three thematic rooms are available for parties. Video games located in the lobby offer a between-game distraction.

☞ **SEASONS AND TIMES**

➛ Year-round: Mon—Thu, 6 pm—10 pm; Fri, 2 pm—midnight; Sat, 10 am—midnight; Sun, 11 am—8 pm. Expanded summer and holiday hours. Reservations required.

☞ **COST**

➛ $7 per 20-minute game or three games for $18. Memberships available. Credit cards accepted.

Laser Trek

7905 FLINT RD. S.E.
CALGARY
(403) 252-9444

Kids six and up are welcome to duck, dodge and skulk their way through more than 12,000 square metres of terrain. Nintendo™ and video games are available in the lobby. Facilities for birthday parties.

☞ **SEASONS AND TIMES**

➛ Year-round: Mon—Thu, 4 pm—10 pm; Fri, 2 pm—midnight; Sat, 10 am—midnight; Sun, 11 am—9 pm. Expanded summer and holiday hours. Reservations required.

☞ **COST**

➛ One game $7, two games $11.50, three games $18. Credit cards accepted.

Paintball & Laser Tag Adventure (PAGE 88)

1912 MACKAY RD. N.W.
CALGARY
(403) 247-8887
WWW.CAPTURETHEFLAG.COM

Kids ages five and up can play in a maze that's just under 3,000 square metres. Birthday parties are held in a somewhat decrepit viewing gallery that doubles as a lounge for the over-18 crowd. Indoor and outdoor paintball adventures are also offered.

SEASONS AND TIMES

→ Year-round: Daily, 10 am—10 pm. Reservations recommended. After-hours access is available on request.

COST

→ $6.50 per 15-minute game, three games for $16.25, eight games or over $5 each. Group specials available. Credit cards accepted.

Make an Ascent INDOOR CLIMBING GYMS

Are your children climbing the walls? Do your toddlers love scaling the furniture? Why not take them to an indoor climbing gym where they can clamber, climb and scramble to their hearts' content. A multitude of routes, suitable for everyone from the novice to the hardcore expert, is available and at most gyms certified instructors are on hand to help children six or older defy gravity safely. Younger children, when accompanied by a parent or guardian, are also welcome and will be delighted with the bouldering caves where no ropes are required and thick crash mats cover the floor. To keep the excitement alive, the routes are altered regularly. Climbing equipment is available for rent, and most gyms have birthday party packages and climbing clubs for thrill-seekers ages six and up.

Calgary Climbing Centre

6 - 7130 Fisher Rd. S.E.
Calgary
(403) 252-6778
www.cadvision.com/calgclimbingctr

The Calgary Climbing Centre offers climbers 120 different routes, a bouldering cave and a traverse wall. Weekend birthday parties can be arranged.

☞ **Seasons and Times**

➛ Summer: Mon—Fri, 3 pm—11 pm; Sat, 10 am—10 pm; Sun, 10 pm—6 pm. Winter: Mon—Fri, noon—midnight; Sat—Sun, 10 am—10 pm.

☞ **Cost**

➛ Adult day pass $11.03, student day pass $10, children's (10 and under) day pass $6. Monthly passes, 10-pass cards and annual memberships available. Harness rental $4, shoe rental $5, carabiner/belay device rental $2, chalk bag and ball rental $2, full rental package $10.

The Stronghold Ltd.

140 - 15th Ave. N.W.
Calgary
(403) 276-6484
www.strongholdclimbing.com

With over 13,500 square metres for climbing, the centre has two children's routes with holds shaped like animals, moons and happy faces that will delight youngsters. Don't let them climb too high—getting down can be harder than going up.

A training room and two bouldering areas, one for beginners to intermediates and the other for advanced climbers, complete the facility. Weekday and weekend birthday parties can be arranged.

☞ Seasons and Times

➛ Summer: Mon–Fri, 3 pm–10 pm; Sat, noon–10 pm; Sun, noon–6 pm. Winter: Mon–Fri, noon–10 pm; Sat, 10 am–8 pm; Sun, 10 am–6 pm.

☞ Cost

➛ Adult day pass $12.15, children's (12 and under) day pass $7.48, bouldering and training rooms only $6.54. Monthly passes, 10-pass cards and annual memberships available. Harness rental $2, shoe rental $4.50, carabiner/grigri rental $1.

University of Calgary Outdoor Program Centre

180 Physical Education Building
Calgary
(403) 220-5038
www.ucalgary.ca/opc

Reservations are recommended here as the climbing wall, which also features a small bouldering cave, can become busy. A separate bouldering wall is located in the basement of the Physical Education building (A-Block). Lessons are available for children as young as ten. Younger kids will find this wall frustrating.

☞ Seasons and Times

➛ Year-round: Mon and Wed–Fri, 8 am–11 pm; Tue, 8 am–7 pm; Sat, 2 pm–8 pm; Sun, 8 am–6 pm. Reduced hours around Christmas. Call ahead to make sure the wall is not being used for a course.

☞ Cost

➛ Adult day pass $5.60, children's (14 and under) day pass $2.40, U of C students and campus recreation members free. A 10-pass card is available. Pass holders will also have access to the fitness centre, pool and Olympic Oval. Harness rental $2, shoe rental $5, carabiner/belay device rental $0.50.

Climbing is also offered at:

Bonkers
3625 Shaganappi Trail N.W. (Market Mall) • (403) 286-7529

Lindsay Park Sports Centre
2225 Macleod Trail S. • (403) 233-8393

Southland Leisure Centre
2000 Southland Dr. S.W. • (403) 251-3505

Bustin' Loose at INDOOR ADVENTURE GYMS

An indoor gym is the perfect place for kids to let off steam any time of the year. While older children run wild in the tube mazes or enjoy the video games, toddlers and crawlers will find an enticing array of playthings, including pint-size slides, ball pits and toys they can ride on. The centres listed below offer birthday party packages. Some have child-minding programs and special activities including sleepovers and playgroups. Each has a cafeteria where adults can kick back with a coffee and biscotti while the younger set refuel on pizza, hot dogs and other kids' favourites.

Note:
Children are required to wear socks at all times.

Bonkers

3625 Shaganappi Trail N.W. (Market Mall)
Calgary
(403) 286-7529

New at Bonkers is its climbing wall. Qualified staff members are on hand to assist your kids to scale the heights.

☞ Year-round: Mon—Fri, 10 am—9 pm; Sat, 9:30 am—9 pm; Sun, 10 am—5 pm. Climbing wall open Fri—Sun. Reduced hours around Christmas. Call to confirm that they're open.

☞ Adults free, children 4 and up $8.39, 18 months to 3 years $6.49, 13 to 17 months $1.99, 12 months and under free. Reduced prices all day Monday, and Wednesdays after 5 pm. Child-minding: $8.39 for the first hour, $4.99 for each subsequent hour (maximum of three hours). Climbing wall: $2 for one climb or $5 for three climbs (includes climbing equipment).

Kid Zone

600 - 3516 – 8TH AVE. N.E. (FRANKLIN MALL)
CALGARY
(403) 273-7529

☞ Year-round: Mon—Tue, 10 am—6 pm; Wed—Sat, 9:30 am—9 pm; Sun, 11 am—6 pm. Reduced hours around Christmas. Call to confirm that they're open.

☞ Adults free, children 5 and up $6.99, 2 to 4 years $4.99, 1 to 2 years $2, 12 months and under free. Reduced prices Mondays and Wednesdays.

Ton of Fun

13266 MACLEOD TRAIL S.E.
CALGARY
(403) 225-4386

2946 – 32ND ST. N.E.
CALGARY
(403) 717-4386

☞ Year-round: Mon—Sat, 9 am—9 pm; Sun, 11 am—6 pm. Reduced hours around Christmas. Call to confirm that they're open.

☞ Adults free, children 3 and up $6.99, 1 to 2 years $3.99, 12 months and under free. Child-minding: $9 for the first hour, $3 for each subsequent hour (maximum of three hours).

Rocky Mountain RAFTING ADVENTURES

Looking for exhilarating adventure amid the breathtaking scenery of the Rockies? Look no further than whitewater rafting. From mild scenic floats suitable for children as young as three, to thrilling half or full-day roller-coaster rides for kids five years and up (over 18 kilograms), outdoor adventure companies in the Calgary area have a tour that's right for your family.

During the trip, professional guides provide direction to paddlers and share their knowledge of local history, flora and fauna. Some companies provide water guns for added fun or make time for an invigorating whitewater swim. Most offer rafting tours combined with other outdoor activities such as mountain biking, caving, hiking or horseback riding. You may also do these activities by themselves.

☞ Seasons and Times

➛ May—Sept, daily (depending on weather and water conditions). Reservations are required.

☞ Cost

➛ Costs vary, but expect to pay at least $39 per adult for a float tour and at least $49 per adult for a whitewater tour. Kids' prices are often slightly cheaper. Prices generally include equipment and wetsuit rental, a professional guide and a lunch or snack when appropriate. On nature floats, binoculars and field guides are generally supplied.

☞ Comment

➛ Dress for the weather of the day and bring a warm sweater, extra socks, sunglasses, a hat, a dry change of clothes and a towel.

Canadian Rockies Rafting
Canmore
1-877-226-7625

Chinook River Sports Ltd.
341 – 10th Ave. S.W.
Calgary
(403) 263-7238 or 1-800-482-4899 • www.chinookraft.com

INSIDE OUT EXPERIENCE LTD.
BRAGG CREEK
(403) 949-3305

MIRAGE ADVENTURE TOURS LTD.
CANMORE
(403) 678-4919 OR 1-888-312-7238 • WWW.MIRAGETOURS.COM

MUKWAH TOURS
14544 MT. MCKENZIE DR. S.E.
CALGARY
(403) 296-0820 OR 1-800-465-0144

OTTER RAFTING ADVENTURES
RED DEER
1-800-661-7379 • WWW.OTTERRAFTING.COM

RAINBOW RIDERS ADVENTURE TOURS
3312 – 3RD AVE. N.W.
CALGARY
(403) 850-3686 • WWW.RAINBOWRIDERS.COM

SUNWEST RIVER GUIDES CO.
4424 - 16TH AVE. N.W.
CALGARY
(403) 276-5388

Just Fore Fun MINIGOLF

If 18 or even 9 holes of regular golf sounds a little overwhelming, get your family hooked on miniature golf instead. Thirty minutes is about all it takes to play a round of 18 holes. The courses offer up old-fashioned fun and have obstacles that can include revolving windmills, cartoon-like animals, tunnels, bridges and even impossibly angled

> **SEASONS AND TIMES**
> → Apr or May—Oct, daily (hours vary).
>
> **COST**
> → Varies, but generally: Adults $6.50, children $4.50.

inclines and crazy roller coaster-like chutes. Other courses, complete with scaled-down sand and water traps, emulate full-size fairways and putting greens. Whichever you visit, the tortuous route the ball must take before it falls into the cup will entrance most kids. Beware, however, some youngsters can become frustrated by a game that looks deceptively simple.

Balls, putters and scorecards are supplied, though keeping score is optional. Birthday parties can be arranged at most of these establishments.

BOWNESS PARK
8900 – 48TH AVE. N.W., CALGARY • (403) 286-9889
CANOE AND PADDLEBOAT RENTALS, SPRAY AND WADING POOLS, PONY RIDES, A MINIATURE TRAIN AND OTHER AMUSEMENT RIDES ARE ALL NEARBY.

KART GARDENS/KART WORLD FAMILY FUN CENTRE
5202 – 1ST ST. S.W., CALGARY • (403) 253-8301
THEY ALSO HAVE GO-CARTS, BUMPER BOATS AND LASER TAG.

PASKAPOO GREENS
88 CANADA OLYMPIC RD., CALGARY • (403) 247-5452
THE OLYMPIC HALL OF FAME AND MUSEUM, A PLAYGROUND, A MOUNTAIN BIKE PARK AND YEAR-ROUND SKI JUMPING ARE ALL NEARBY.

PRAIRIE WINDS DRIVING RANGE & MINIATURE GOLF
33 CASTLERIDGE BLVD. N.E., CALGARY • (403) 285-7770
A PLAYGROUND, A SPRAY POOL AND A WADING POOL ARE ALL NEARBY.

TARGET GREENS GOLF CENTRE
1851 – 84TH ST. N.E., CALGARY • (403) 285-2009

TEE TO GREEN SPORTS LTD.
MACLEOD TRAIL AND SHAWNESSY BLVD. S.W., CALGARY • (403) 256-7447

Carving Turns at WINTERGREEN GOLF AND SKI RESORT

BRAGG CREEK
(403) 949-5100

Looking for new ways to enjoy winter outdoors with your clan? A day at Wintergreen Golf and Ski Resort will cure cabin fever and leave the whole family smiling. While snowboarders "bust huge air" in the new 1.2-hectare terrain park, novice and intermediate skiers can explore the centre's 11 downhill runs. A gently sloped bunny hill that has a magic carpet lift inspires confidence in youngsters and other first-time skiers, while a slightly steeper hill with a rope tow will challenge more confident beginners. Five kilometres of trackset trails are available to cross-country skiers.

When your brood tires of skiing, strap on

☞ SEASONS AND TIMES

➛ Summer: Apr—Oct, daily, 6 am—sundown.
Winter: Nov—Mar or Apr, daily, Mon—Tue and Sun, 9 am—4 pm; Wed—Sat, 9 am—9 pm.
Tube park and cross-country skiing: Mon—Thu, call for hours; Fri, 5 pm—9 pm; Sat, noon—9 pm; Sun, noon—4 pm.

☞ COST

➛ Skiing and snowboarding: Individuals (13 and up) $15, seniors and children (6 to 12) $10, under 6 free.
Cross-country skiing: Individuals (13 and up) $4, seniors and children (6 to 12) $3, under 6 free.
Magic carpet and rope tow only: Individuals (6 and over) $5, under 6 free.
Tube park: $5 per person.
Fitness and climbing wall: Individuals (6 and over) $8.
Discounted admission and rentals two hours before closing. Season's passes available. Credit cards accepted.

everyone's skates and head to the small outdoor skating rink (free), or grab an inner tube for an exhilarating spin through the tube park.

Equipment rentals and ski and snowboarding instruction are available, including a parent-and-tot program. There is a daycare for children 19 months and up. Wintergreen also has a fitness centre and an indoor climbing wall and, in summer, offers visitors an 18-hole golf course, a driving range and an outdoor swimming pool.

Getting There

- By car, take Centre St. north to 6th Ave. S.W. (its name changes to Bow Trail) and go west. Turn south on Sarcee Trail, then west on Hwy. 8 (Glenmore Trail). At Hwy. 22 turn south and continue to Bragg Creek. At Bragg Creek turn west onto Balsam Ave., then north on Wintergreen Rd. Watch for signs on your left. Free parking on site. About 45 minutes from the Calgary Tower.
- By public transit, buses depart regularly from various points around the city. Call 949-5100 for a schedule.

Similar Attraction

- **Canada Olympic Park,** 88 Canada Olympic Rd. N.W., Calgary (403) 247-5452.

Kiddies' Play Areas
McDONALD'S™ AND BURGER KING™

Kids need to be kids, even when it's pouring outside. Take them to a McDonald's™ or Burger King™ play area and they can have all the fun they like—without you even making a food purchase. Both restaurants' play areas feature brightly coloured tunnels, slides, ball pits and punching bags, though size and layout will vary from outlet to outlet. For the Nintendo™ aficionado, some McDonald's™ restaurants feature interactive computer games.

SEASONS AND TIMES
→ Year-round: Daily (hours vary with the restaurant).

COST
→ Play areas: Free (meals extra).

Wherever you go, tables located either inside or adjacent to the glassed-in play area allow parents to enjoy the fun. And if your kids do stop long enough to eat, both chains offer kid-size meals that come with a toy. Disposable bibs and highchairs are available and the place mats can be coloured, so bring crayons. Birthday parties can be arranged.

NORTHEAST CALGARY

BURGER KING
100 – 52ND ST. N.E. • (403) 215-8099

McDONALD'S
5219 FALSBRIDGE GATE N.E. • (403) 293-4052

INTERACTIVE COMPUTER GAMES AT:
3660 - 12 AVE. N.E. • (403) 273-1219
2740 – 32ND AVE. N.E. • (403) 291-0256

NORTHWEST CALGARY

BURGER KING
11 CROWFOOT TERRACE N.W. • (403) 215-1008

McDONALD'S
6820 – 4TH ST. N.W. • (403) 295-1004
63 CROWFOOT WAY N.W. • (403) 241-1785

SOUTHEAST CALGARY

BURGER KING
14900 DEER RIDGE DR. S.E. • (403) 215-1005

McDONALD'S
20 RIVERGLEN DR. S.E. • (403) 236-4122

INTERACTIVE COMPUTER GAMES AT:
13780 BOW BOTTOM TRAIL S.E. • (403) 271-7411
248 MIDPARK WAY S.E. • (403) 256-0656
4615 – 17TH AVE. S.E. • (403) 272-7477

SOUTHWEST CALGARY
BURGER KING
7110 MACLEOD TRAIL S. • (403) 215-1002
10400 MACLEOD TRAIL S. • (403) 215-1010

Sandy Swimming and WADING BEACHES

In Calgary, most water comes straight from the snow-bound peaks of the nearby Rocky Mountains. It's ice-cold, but your kids won't mind. So pack up their beach towels, swimsuits and sand toys and head out for a day of fun at the beach.

At the river sites listed below, kids will find plenty of small stones for skipping or throwing, larger ones for building dams and forts, and there are all kinds of fascinating minnows for catching or just observing up close. Grassy banks provide parents with pleasant places to sit and take in the surroundings. At Lake Sikome the water is warmer than at the river sites and there's a sandy beach with swimming that's supervised.

Toilets, playgrounds, picnic tables and concession stands (with the noted exception) are found near all three sites. Keep in mind that Calgary's swollen rivers can be dangerous during spring thaw.

STANLEY PARK (RIVER SITE)
4011 - 1A ST. S.W.
CALGARY

SANDY BEACH (RIVER SITE)
CALGARY
(NO FOOD CONCESSION)
FOLLOW 50TH AVE. S.W.

LAKE SIKOME (LAKE SITE)
FISH CREEK PROVINCIAL PARK
CALGARY
FOLLOW BOW BOTTOM TRAIL S.E.

Great Tobogganing RUNS

Snowfall can be variable in Calgary—but when it finally does appear, the toboggans come out in droves. And why not? What could be more exhilarating than swooping down a powdery slope, eyes half-closed against the wind and the icy lashings of flying snow? What could be more companionable than swapping "close call" stories on the long trudge back up? In that spirit, here's a list of popular tobogganing runs throughout Calgary.

NORTHEAST CALGARY

PRAIRIE WINDS PARK
OFF CASTLERIDGE BLVD. N.E.

MONTEREY PARK
OFF CATALINA BLVD. (BETWEEN CALIFORNIA BLVD. AND 26TH AVE. N.E.)

DEERFOOT PARK
1604 – 14TH AVE. N.E.

MARLBOROUGH PARK COMMUNITY ASSOCIATION
6021 MADIGAN DR. N.E.

NORTHWEST CALGARY

CONFEDERATION PARK
OFF 10TH ST. N.W. (NORTH END OF THE PARK)

SOUTHEAST CALGARY

ERIN WOODS
20 Erin Woods Dr. S.E.

MAPLE RIDGE
Off Maple Ridge Close S.E.

SOUTHWEST CALGARY

KINGSLAND
Off Heritage Dr. S.W. (behind the Jimmie Condon/Rose Kohn Arenas)

RIVER PARK
Off 14A St. (between 39th Ave. and 42nd Ave. S.W.)

RICHMOND GREEN
At 33rd Ave. and 25th St. S.W.

SIGNAL RIDGE
At Sirocco Dr. and Signal Hill Heights S.W.

STANLEY PARK
4011 1A St. S.W.

STRATHCONA PARK
277 Strathcona Dr. S.W.

Chapter 5

Places to Learn

Introduction

When learning happens out-of-doors, on a family field trip or with the help of some nifty interactive displays, it doesn't feel like learning at all. In this chapter, you'll discover some great ways to sneak a bit of education into your child's day, without interrupting the fun. At the *Calgary Sun*, your kids can join reporters, photographers and editors as they bring home the daily news. At other sites, they'll learn all kinds of facts about fish, watch a bronze sculpture take shape or delve into the lives led by German prisoners of war. There's also the Ann and Sandy Cross Conservation area, where children can investigate the animals and plants that call the foothills home. Or pack a picnic lunch, head to the woods and spend some time absorbing the in's and out's of forest management. Shh! Just don't tell them these outings are educational.

Stop the Presses! THE CALGARY SUN

**2615 - 12th St. N.E.
Calgary
(403) 250-4265**

Every day the newspaper is delivered to your door—ever wondered what goes on behind the scenes? Why not tour one of Calgary's daily newspapers and find out?

Children ages five and older can observe the activity in the Calgary Sun building, where everything from taking ads to writing articles to printing goes on during the day. Take the one hour guided tour, and your kids will discover how an editor alters the front page as the news day unfolds. They'll also join photographers and reporters as they monitor police scanners to find pictures and stories, and see the massive rolls of paper used in the presses. But the highlight of the trip for most youngsters is the presses themselves, which can print up to 25,000

Seasons and Times
→ Year-round: Mon–Fri, 9 am–5 pm.

Cost
→ Free.

Getting There
→ By car, take 9th Ave. east to Macleod Trail and go north. Turn east on 5th Ave., stay to the right and head east on Memorial Dr. At Deerfoot Trail head north to 32nd Ave. N.E. and go east. Turn south on 12th St. N.E. and continue to the Calgary Sun. Free parking on site. About 15 minutes from the Calgary Tower.

→ By public transit, take the Whitehorn LRT to Rundle Station. Transfer to CT bus 32 and take it to 12th St. and 27th Ave. N.E.

Comment
→ Groups of eight or more may book guided tours about three months in advance.

Similar Attraction
→ **Calgary Herald**, 215 - 16 St. S.E., Calgary (403) 235-7100.

copies of the paper an hour. And though they're not always running, stationary presses mean you can get a closer look at the massive machines.

It's about Trees and Escapees
BARRIER LAKE FIELD STATION

Off Hwy. 40
Kananaskis
(403) 220-5355

At the University of Calgary's Barrier Lake Field Station, your children can learn about forest ecology, forest management and even local history. During the Second World War, this site was a prisoner of war camp for captured German officers, and the remains of Camp 130 are there for visitors to see.

Three interpretive trails (the Barrier Lake Forestry Trails) wind through the area. The History Loop (0.3 kilometres) takes visitors to an old guard tower and to the Colonel's cabin, where there are pictures of the camp as it was in

Seasons and Times

➛ Mid-May—Labour Day: Daily. Interpretive staff are available on weekends.
Trails are open year-round, but are not maintained in the winter.

Cost

➛ Free.

Getting There

➛ By car, take Centre St. north to 6th Ave. S.W. (its name changes to Bow Trail) and go west. Turn north on Sarcee Trail, then west on Hwy. 1. At Hwy. 40 turn south and continue to the Kananaskis Field Station turnoff. Free parking on site. About 50 minutes from the Calgary Tower.

the 1940s. Kids can learn about various daring escape attempts. Signs along the loop provide information about the lives of German officers as well as the guards and staff who lived here.

The Forest Ecology Loop (1.5 kilometres) is an interpretive nature walk that teaches visitors about the ecology of local forest communities, while the Forestry Loop has signs explaining how the need for timber is balanced with conservation. Additional signs along both trails help youngsters with plant identification. The small interpretive centre at the trailhead has displays about forests for kids. They can count the rings on a tree and learn about the role bacteria, fungi, insects, animals and plants play in forest ecosystems.

Studio West
BRONZE FOUNDRY AND ART GALLERY

205 - 2ND AVE. S.E.
COCHRANE
(403) 932-2611

Western Canada's first fine art bronze foundry gives older children the opportunity to learn about the lost method of wax casting, a process that dates back over 3,000 years. Using a small bronze sculpture as

> **SEASONS AND TIMES**
> ➛ Year-round: Daily, 9 am–5 pm.
>
> **COST**
> ➛ Free.

☞ **Getting There**

➛ By car, take Centre St. north to 6th Ave. S.W. (its name changes to Bow Trail) and go west. Turn north on Sarcee Trail, then west on Hwy. 1. At Hwy. 22 turn north, continue to the bridge and turn east on Griffin Rd. At 2nd Ave. E. turn north for one block. Free parking on site. About 45 minutes from the Calgary Tower.

☞ **Comment**

➛ Some of the site is wheelchair accessible. Plan a 1-hour visit.

a teaching tool, staff at the foundry take visitors through the many stages of the process, from the creation of a rubber mold to finishing, in which the bright new bronze is given its characteristic aged look. Afterwards, your family will have the opportunity to view the pieces already completed by the foundry and awaiting shipment to corporations and private collectors around the world. Maquette or scale models of several sculptures made at the foundry, many of which have horses as their subject, can also be viewed. Children with an artistic bent will enjoy looking at how, through the use of texture and other means, different artists have represented the horse in a variety of ways.

The foundry's enlarging area is included in the tour. Here, foundry staff can make a larger copy of an artist's sculpture. Of all the stages involved in the process, the actual casting is both the most spectacular and the shortest, taking only minutes (other stages may take weeks to complete). Those wishing to see the bronze poured should call ahead for details.

Fascinating Fish Facts SAM LIVINGSTON FISH HATCHERY

1440-17A St. S.E.
Calgary
(403) 297-6561

This completely enclosed fish hatchery is the first of its kind in North America. Within its temperature-controlled tanks of water, up to 3.5 million trout are reared throughout the year before eventually being released into Alberta's lakes and streams. Both guided and self-guided tours of the facility are available and include an opportunity to see, from large viewing windows, how the fish are raised from tiny eggs to fingerlings 10 to 15 centimetres long. Other exhibits include a display of the automated feeders used in the hatchery, a guide to the identification of various fish species, and there's even an interactive model of a trout's basic body parts. Guided tours also feature a short, age-appropriate video.

While school-age children will get the most out

Seasons and Times

→ Summer: Mon–Fri, 10 am–4 pm; weekends and holidays, 1 pm–5 pm. Winter: Mon–Fri, 10 am–4 pm.

Cost

→ Free, donations appreciated. A $20 refundable tour confirmation cheque is required to book a tour.

Getting There

→ By car, take 9th Ave. east to 19th St. S.E. and turn left. Cross Blackfoot Trail (19th St. changes to 17A St. at this point) and follow the signs to the hatchery. Free parking on site. About ten minutes from the Calgary Tower.

→ By public transit, take CT bus 1 to 9th Ave. and 17th St. S.E. and walk the three blocks to the hatchery.

☞ **NEARBY**
➛Pearce Estate Park.

☞ **COMMENT**
➛Groups of ten or more may book guided tours about two months in advance. Plan a 90-minute visit for both the self-guided and guided tours.

of the visit, the activity in the hatchery and many of the displays will appeal to younger children as well. When they do begin to fidget, take them downstairs, where aquariums provide a closer look at the various species of trout raised in the hatchery. Depending on the size of your group and any other groups visiting, youngsters may be invited into the back area to feed the always-voracious trout.

An Education in Trees
JUMPINGPOUND DEMONSTRATION FOREST

OFF HWY. 68 (SIBBALD CREEK TRAIL)
(403) 297-8800

Did you know that about 40 percent of Alberta's forests are contained in protected areas like parks, ecological reserves and wilderness areas? Of the remaining woodlands, some are managed by the forest industry. At the Jumpingpound Demonstration Forest, children will learn how this indus-

☞ **SEASONS AND TIMES**
➛ May—Oct, daily. In winter the road is closed to cars, though you may walk, snowshoe or ski the route.

☞ **COST**
➛ Free.

try works to balance its own needs with those of the environment.

Stop first at the open-air interpretive centre, where kids can view displays on the history of the Demonstration Forest and learn about some of the management practices they'll see along the 10-kilometre self-guided tour that you'll do in your car. Before you leave, pick up brochures for the auto tour and Forest walking trails.

> **☞ GETTING THERE**
> ➛ By car, take Centre St. north to 6th Ave. S.W. (its name changes to Bow Trail) and go west. Turn north on Sarcee Trail, then west on Hwy. 1. At Hwy. 68 turn south and continue for 18 kilometres to the Forest turnoff. Free parking on site. About 40 minutes from the Calgary Tower.
>
> **☞ COMMENT**
> ➛ Plan a 1-hour visit for the auto tour, more if you decide to walk the trails. Not all parts of this site are wheelchair accessible.

There are ten stops along the auto tour that demonstrate the different stages in the 80-year cycle of a managed forest. Among other things, kids will learn how reserve stands are left for watershed protection, wildlife habitat and other uses. They will also see how trees are pruned and thinned and how the ground is prepared for seeding.

When energetic youngsters need to stretch their legs, head to the Forest's walking trails: the four-kilometre Pine Woods Loop winds through a stand of pines that was machine-planted in 1974. There's also a short wetlands trail and the Moose Creek Loop, an interpretive walking trail that meanders through forests of varying maturity. Numbered posts mark features of interest along the path. The trailhead's day use area is perfect for a picnic lunch.

A Walk on the Wild Side
THE ANN AND SANDY CROSS CONSERVATION AREA

Off Hwy. 22X
Calgary
(403) 931-2042

Ann and Sandy Cross donated over 1,900 hectares of foothills land to help establish the Cross Conservation Area. Designed to protect habitat and educate visitors about preservation and conservation, the area has over 20 kilometres of trails winding through aspen forest, introduced grasses and native prairie.

Education stations along two self-guided interpretive trails, the Fescue Trail and the Chevron Aspen Trail, introduce children to some of the land's inhabitants, such as coyotes, elk, deer, moose, porcupine, great-horned owls and red-tailed hawks. Try to spot and name the beautiful wildflowers that grow in the area. A gravel trail that's seasonal is

☞ Seasons and Times
➛ Year-round: Daily, dawn–dusk. Visits must be booked at least one day in advance. Call 931-2042.

☞ Cost
➛ Free.

☞ Getting There
➛ By car, take 9th Ave. east to 1st St. S.E. (its name changes to Macleod Trail) and go south. Turn west on Hwy. 22X and continue to the Calgary city limits sign. Take the first left onto 160th St. The conservation area parking lot is at the top of the hill. About 45 minutes from the Calgary Tower.

☞ Comment
➛ Trails (most are loops) range in length from 2 to 8.7 kilometres and only one is wheelchair and stroller accessible. Horses, dogs and other pets are not allowed in the conservation area. Plan at least a 2-hour visit.

suitable for strollers and wheelchairs and leads to a spectacular panoramic view of the surrounding foothills.

Many of the trails are in full sun so bring sunscreen and a hat for everyone; you'll also want mosquito repellent and plenty of water. Special programs offer children and families the chance to explore the lives of insects, learn about bats, scan the sky for raptors, or make a water scope to investigate the area's pond life. Nature safari summer day camps are offered to children ages 6 to 12. In the winter, you can learn about animal tracks or sign up for a fun-filled day of winter nature activities.

Chapter 6

Music, Theatre, Dance and Cinema

Introduction

The world of the arts has a tremendous amount to offer children. Performing arts such as theatre, music and dance open their minds to all kinds of imaginative ideas and possibilities. In Calgary, some theatre and dance companies, such as Quest and Decidedly Jazz Danceworks, make a point of visiting schools and mounting programs especially for kids. At other theatres, such as Storybook, children are the performers. Loose Moose Theatre, renowned for its Theatresports, is improv-based and its children's matinees allow the kids in the audience to call out responses to what's happening on-stage.

Dance schools often present recitals that are a good way to introduce dance to youngsters. If your children get extremely restless, your family can leave and you won't regret having spent $100 on tickets. Consider performances at the University of Calgary for older kids—only be sure to find out whether the play is suitable for children.

Your children may be so taken with a particular performing art that they'll want to learn how to do it themselves. Many of the following venues offer acting or dance classes as well.

Take to the Stage with STORYBOOK THEATRE

(403) 216-0808
WWW.STORYBOOKTHEATRE.ORG

Storybook Theatre is an established company specializing in entertaining kids. It operates out of the Pumphouse Theatre (2140 Pumphouse Ave. S.W.) and Crescent Heights Community Centre (1101 – 2nd St. N.W.; 276-1002). The company presents eight plays per season, often with child actors in their casts. Storybook's Cookie Cabaret Series, presented at Crescent Heights, is geared toward kids aged three to seven, while its Adventure Series, presented at the Pumphouse, is aimed at older kids, seven and up.

Storybook's other programs include Sleepovers in the Theatre (one for each of its Adventure Plays); and Summer Drama Day Camps (Fairytale Summer for ages six to eight; Shakespeare in the Summer for ages 9 to 13; and Greek Tales for ages 13 to 17). Around Christmas a carolling troupe and Cabaret

☞ SEASONS AND TIMES

➛ Oct–May.
Cookie Cabaret: Sat, 11 am and 1:30 pm; Sun, 12:30 pm and 3 pm.
Adventure Series: Wed–Fri, 7:30 pm; Sat–Sun, noon and 3:30 pm.

☞ COST

➛ Cookie Cabaret: $6.
Adventure Theatre: $6 to $14. Cheaper for weekday performances.

on the Road (touring Cookie Cabaret plays) perform for company parties and other large events.

You'll want to get a good seat, so book as early as possible; seasons' passes are sold between May and October for the upcoming season.

☞ Getting There

Crescent Heights Community Centre:

➛ Take Centre St. north to 5th Ave. and then turn east, following 5th until it turns into Edmonton Trail. Drive north on Edmonton Trail to 12th Ave. and turn west, crossing Centre St. Two blocks later, turn south on 2nd St. and into the Crescent Heights High School (free) parking lot; across from the parking lot is the centre. About 15 minutes from the Calgary Tower.

➛ By public transit, take CT bus 2 (Mount Pleasant) eastbound from 5th Ave. and 2nd St. S.W. to 12th Ave. and 2nd St. N.W. Walk south from there.

➛ By bicycle or on foot, follow the directions for car.

Pumphouse Theatre:

➛ By car, take 9th Ave. east to Macleod Trail and turn north onto 4th Ave. Drive west on 4th to Bow Trail and continue west, watching for signs directing you to the Pumphouse Theatre. Take the Pumphouse turn-off northwest and turn north onto Pumphouse Ave. The theatre is on your right. Free parking on site and along the street. About ten minutes from the Calgary Tower.

➛ No buses or C-trains go to the Pumphouse.

➛ By bicycle or on foot, take 9th Ave. west to 11th St. Turn north and cross Bow Trail using the bike paths and following the signs to the Pumphouse.

☞ Comment

➛ Both theatres have first aid kits but not trained personnel. If you will need wheelchair or stroller access at the Pumphouse, please call Storybook and inform staff in advance of the performance.

Conducting Kids at THE CALGARY PHILHARMONIC ORCHESTRA

Arts Centre
205 - 8th Ave. S.E.
Calgary
(403) 571-0849
www.htn.com/cpo

Like most orchestras these days, the Calgary Philharmonic Orchestra (CPO) knows it's important to introduce classical music early to those whom it hopes will be its future patrons. To that end, it makes itself accessible to schools and entices children to certain of its concerts at its home, the Art Centre's Jack Singer Concert Hall. The Esso Kids Program presents Saturday Morning at the Symphony, six popular events during the season, with demonstrations and music making. These gatherings start with a lively 30-minute presentation by the musicians and conductors with questions from the audience, then continue with the first half of a Light Classics Dress Rehearsal.

☞ Seasons and Times

➛ Regular season: Sept—mid-June.
Saturday Morning at the Symphony: Sat, 9:15 am.
Young People's Series: Selected Saturdays, 2 pm.
Education Series: Days vary, 10 am.

☞ Cost

➛ Saturday Morning tickets (series of three only): Adults $17 to $21, children and students $15.
Young People's Concert Series (per ticket): Adults $17 to $21, children and students $12 to $15.
The Education Series: $4.50 per student. One ticket free for an adult accompanying ten paid students.
Full-time students (high school or post-secondary) can take in five Friday Classic Concerts for $50 (call 571-0849 for tickets).

☞ GETTING THERE

➛ The Arts Centre is two blocks east of the Calgary Tower. By car, proceed east on 9th Ave. past Macleod Trail and park in the pay lot underneath the Municipal Building. Cross Macleod to the Arts Centre.

➛ By public transit, take the downtown LRT to the City Hall stop on the south side of 7th Ave. or the Olympic Plaza stop on the north, then walk south on Macleod Trail to 8th Ave. and turn west to get to Singer Hall, at the west end of the Arts Centre. CT buses 10, 9, 4 and 31 all stop at the Municipal Building.

☞ NEARBY

➛ Olympic Plaza, W.R. Castell Public Library, Municipal Building, Glenbow Museum, Stephen Avenue Mall, Calgary Police Service Interpretive Centre.

☞ COMMENT

➛ Why not arrive early and watch the musicians tune up their instruments? Please mention wheelchair requirements at time of booking.

The Renaissance Energy Young People's Series (matinees intended for school-aged children) is a group of imaginative Saturday afternoon concerts where kids might learn about great composers, or enjoy a mix of music on an animal theme and an informative chat by someone from the Calgary Zoo. Puppeteers are sometimes enlisted to animate the classics and occasionally geographical tours are conducted via rhythm and melody. Before the concerts begin, there's a musical Petting Zoo, where children and musicians meet and kids are allowed to "pet" the instruments.

The CPO's Education Series is meant for elementary school students, and is integrated with the schools' curriculum.

Canadian Cartoons NATIONAL FILM BOARD RENTALS

W.R. Castell Central Library
616 Macleod Trail S.E.
Calgary
(403) 260-2600
http://public-library.calgary.ab.ca

Oh, Canada! We're animation giants. But you'd hardly know it from the subtle presence National Film Board (NFB) releases have after their very first, understated run. Luckily, some of the NFB's great films and shorts are available, though, through the W.R. Castell Public Library downtown and at other libraries around town (page 73). The Castell library has the largest selection, but you can order a favourite title through your local branch and keep it for seven days. You'll find classics such as *The Snit*, *Blackberry Subway Jam* (based on a book by Robert Munsch), *The Man Who Planted Trees* and *Snow Cat*—brilliant works that put much of the stuff on television to shame. The library also has non-commercial videos about animals, videos based on

☞ Seasons and Times

→ Castell library: Mon—Thu, 10 am—9 pm; Fri—Sat, 10 am—5 pm; Sun, 1:30 pm—5 pm.

☞ Cost

→ Children's library card, free. Adult library card, $10 per year.

☞ Getting There

→ By car, take 9th Ave. east to Macleod Trail and turn north. The library is two blocks down on the corner of 7th Ave. S.E. Look for pay parking in the area. Minutes from the Calgary Tower.

→ By public transit, take CT buses 10, 9, 4 or 31 to the Municipal Building and cross 7th Ave. Or, take the downtown train to City Hall Station. It's across the avenue from the library.

→ By bicycle or on foot, use the car directions.

Nearby
➛ Arts Centre, Calgary Tower, Calgary Police Service Interpretive Centre, Olympic Plaza.

Comment
➛ The Castell library has a reasonably large supply of French-language videos, including NFB titles.

books, and how-to craft videos.

While at any library, be sure to pick up a schedule of events. Story times, film screenings and information sessions featuring guests from such interesting spots as the Calgary Zoo are going on all the time. Check out the Web site above, too, for schedules.

Zany Hijinks at LOOSE MOOSE THEATRE COMPANY

1229 - 9TH AVE. S.E.
CALGARY
(403) 265-5682
WWW.LOOSEMOOSE.COM

Loose Moose Theatre's funny, accessible Theatresports—improv theatre presented in a competitive set-up—put it on the map back in the 1970s and the company continues to present Theatresports evenings on a regular basis. However, these tend to be more adult-oriented than not, so save Theatresports until your child's

Seasons and Times
➛ Sept—Apr, Sat—Sun, 1 and 3 pm. Call for exact dates.

Cost
➛ $6 per person.
Group rates available for ten or more.

adolescence or later, when they will probably be absolutely delighted by its freewheeling format.

Children, on the other hand, get a big kick out of the company's improv-based style when it's applied to stories for them. Loose Moose presents four children's plays per season (four weekends each) for kids ages four to ten, featuring cheerful presentations with plenty of good humour. The shows are presented at Inglewood's Garry Theatre, and the neighbourhood itself is an interesting place for a stroll before or after the play. While the company doesn't organize birthday parties, there's nothing stopping you from taking your child's friends to the play and then doing cake and presents elsewhere. Some families choose to repair to Spolumbo's (1308 - 9th Ave. S.E.; 264-6452) after the performance, where they can eat panini and open gifts in a semi-private area.

☞ GETTING THERE

➛ By car, take 9th Ave. east to 12th St. and park in the area, at a meter or in a public lot. About ten minutes from the Calgary Tower.

➛ By public transit, take CT bus 1 (Forest Lawn) at 8th Ave. and Centre St. It will let you off near the Garry Theatre.

➛ By bike or on foot, use the car directions.

☞ NEARBY

➛ Calgary Zoo, Deane House Historic Site & Restaurant, Pearce Estate Park, Inglewood Bird Sanctuary.

☞ COMMENT

➛ This could be a good follow-up after a brief visit to the zoo or the Inglewood Bird Sanctuary.

Jazz It Up at DECIDEDLY JAZZ DANCEWORKS

1514 - 4TH ST. S.W.
CALGARY
(403) 245-3533
WWW.DECIDEDLYJAZZ.COM

This Calgary jazz dance company mounts engaging productions which may not be aimed at children but are almost always up a kid's alley. The troupe's hallmark is exuberant and accessible dancing—there's nothing deliberately obscure happening onstage. The music the company uses, which is sometimes performed live and sometimes not, is often infectious, and the choreography is inspired by dance from cultures around the world. Artistic director Vicki Adams Willis has a fondness for funny, clownish dance works and there is often at least one gracing any given program. Children who dance themselves are most likely to enjoy DJD, and others who are exposed to this accomplished company may well find themselves looking for further exposure to jazz dance.

Productions take place at different venues around town, including the Martha Cohen Theatre at the Arts Centre and the Uptown

☞ SEASONS AND TIMES
➛ Fall—Spring: Call the DJD office for information.

☞ COST
➛ Adults $14 to $25, students and seniors $11.50 to $20.

☞ COMMENT
➛ Feel free to call the DJD office and ask if a show is suitable for the children you plan to take with you. Very young children should probably not attend.

Theatre. Make sure to note where the company is performing before heading out, as the address above is DJD's studio address, not its performing space. DJD also offers dance classes and school programs.

Sing, Sing Out Loud
THE CALGARY OPERA

601 - 237 - 8TH AVE. S.E.
CALGARY
(403) 299-8888
WWW.CALGARYOPERA.CA

Heroes, heroines, revenge, romance and tragedy—sounds like the stuff of Saturday morning cartoons, but these heady elements have also always distinguished the plots at the opera. The Calgary Opera offers all kinds of exciting stories to the adventurous family, and anyone who's enthusiastic about classical music will have the edge when it comes to appreciating this art form, presented at the Jubilee.

One way to pique a child's interest is to attend an annual Opera Look-in, a free family event where members of the public are invited for a behind-the-scenes look at opera production. This one-hour tour includes meeting the cast and crew responsible for the lavish spectacles. Enjoy the afternoon tour, then see the show, or vice versa. The more education chil-

☞ SEASONS AND TIMES
➛ Oct—Mar. Check the current program for details.

☞ COST
➛ Single ticket: $13 to $77. Discounted seating sections for youths. Subscriptions are available.

☞ **GETTING THERE**

➛ By car, take 9th Ave. east to Centre St. and turn north. Turn west onto 4th Ave. and continue west to 10th St. Turn north on 10th, then west onto Kensington Rd. Drive west to 14th St., then turn north. The Jubilee is at the top of the hill on your right. Turn east, then south, to get to the main parking lot. About 15 minutes from the Calgary Tower.

➛ By public transit, take CT bus 10 (Market Mall) from 6th Ave. and 2nd St. S.W. and ride it to 14th St. and 14th Ave. N.W. Or, take the Brentwood train from 7th Ave. and 1st St. S.W. to the SAIT/Jubilee Station.

☞ **NEARBY**

➛ Peters Drive-In, SAIT, University of Calgary.

☞ **COMMENT**

➛ There's a first aid kit on-site and some Jubilee staff are trained.

dren have before watching their first opera, the better—familiarity with the music and storyline will go a long way toward helping them savour the experience.

The Calgary Opera tries to make itself accessible to schools. For Students Only allows teachers, equipped with study guides, to take their students to dress rehearsals ($5 per ticket). BP Amoco Let's Create An Opera is a program that gives students the chance to write, stage and perform their own operas.

To reach Calgary Opera administration to discuss the appropriateness of material for children, call 262-7286.

All the World's a Stage THE SHAKESPEARE COMPANY

306 JACKSON PLACE N.W.
CALGARY
(403) 289-3680
WWW.SHAKESPEARECOMPANY.COM

The Shakespeare Company specializes in, you guessed it, the works of the Bard and though it doesn't aim most of them at children, some kids will find some of these classic plays approachable. Be sure to call ahead to find out whether a particular production is suitable for the child you have in mind, and do as much preparation as you can (there are books a-plenty on Shakespeare for kids; try your local library). The company's shows are presented in the Pumphouse Theatre (2140 Pumphouse Ave. S.W.). Certain plays feature student matinees for older children to see with their school classes. Sometimes there are productions for younger kids (E.C.S. level to grade 6).

☞ SEASONS AND TIMES

→ Nov–May, Tue–Sat, 7:30 pm. Call 263-0079 for specific dates and tickets.

☞ COST

→ Adults $13, seniors and students $7. Tickets are half price on Tuesday nights.

☞ GETTING THERE

→ By car, take 9th Ave. east to Macleod Trail and turn north. Turn west onto 4th Ave., and proceed to Bow Trail. Continue west along Bow Trail, watching for signs directing you to the Pumphouse Theatre. Take the Pumphouse turnoff northwest and turn north onto Pumphouse Ave. The theatre is on your right. Free parking on site and along the street. About 10 minutes from the Calgary Tower.

→ No buses or C-trains go to the Pumphouse.

→ By bicycle or on foot, take 9th Ave. west to 11th St. Turn north and cross Bow Trail using the bike paths and following the signs to the Pumphouse.

☞ COMMENT

→ The theatre has a first aid kit but no trained personnel. If you will need wheelchair access at the Pumphouse, please call The Shakespeare Company and inform staff in advance of the performance.

Dance Your Heart Out at ALBERTA BALLET

141 - 18TH AVE. S.W.
(403) 299-8888
CALGARY
WWW.ALBERTABALLET.COM

This professional ballet company presents a season of performances at the Jubilee every year, one of the most popular of which is that holiday staple, *The Nutcracker*. This compelling story with seasonal glitter and bits of magic is a great way to introduce children to dance. The Alberta Ballet generally presents more contemporary works than story ballets, which tend to be staged here by touring troupes, such as the National and Royal Winnipeg Ballets.

A cheaper way to introduce your youngsters to ballet is to attend one of the company's choreographic shows, where dancers in the troupe create pieces and their peers perform them. (Cheaper still is attending productions by local dance schools, but the calibre of dance there will not be as professional.)

For information on productions that are suitable for children, call the ballet's administration (245-4222). Arrive at performances early so you can go through the program

☞ **SEASONS AND TIMES**
➛ Oct—May. Call for showtimes.

☞ **COST**
➛ From $17.50 to $52.50. Discounts for children, students and seniors in the mid-range prices of tickets.

☞ **GETTING THERE**
➛ By car, take 9th Ave. east to Centre St. and turn north. Turn west onto 4th Ave. and continue west to 10th St. Turn north on 10th, then west onto Kensington Rd. Drive west to 14th St., then turn north. The Jubilee is at the top of the hill on your right. Turn east, then south, to get to the main parking lot. About 15 minutes from the Calgary Tower.
➛ By public transit, take CT bus 10 (Market Mall) from 6th Ave. and 2nd St. S.W. and ride it to 14th St. and 14th Ave. N.W. Or, take the Brentwood train from 7th Ave. and 1st St. S.W. to the SAIT/Jubilee Station.

with your children and help them understand what they are about to see, and take money for a snack or drink at intermission to buck up flagging attention spans.

☞ **NEARBY**
➛ Peters Drive-In, SAIT, University of Calgary.

☞ **COMMENT**
➛ There's a first aid kit on-site and some Jubilee staff are trained.

Edifying Entertainment
IMAX™ THEATRE

EAU CLAIRE MARKET
CALGARY
(403) 974-4646

The technology that produced the first IMAX™ film has proven itself a boon to entertaining children. The gigantic screen at Eau Claire's IMAX™ Theatre can't fail to engage the viewer of any age, and most of the films that play there centre around family-friendly themes such as animals and other aspects of nature. Sharks in the wild, wolves in their habitat, an expedition on Mount Everest, a remake of Fantasia . . . each of these subjects has had IMAX™ treatment.

The other benefit of the IMAX™ format is that most films last about 45 minutes, which jibes

☞ **SEASONS AND TIMES**
➛ Matinees and evening shows: Daily. Closed Christmas Day. Call the theatre for times.

☞ **COST**
➛ Single and double bill: General (13 to 59) $8.50 and $12, seniors (60 and over) $7.50 and $11, children (12 and under) $6.50 and $10. Group rates available for 20 or more, call 974-4622.

perfectly with the attention span of younger kids. In addition, IMAX™ offers all the accoutrements of the North American movie-going experience—popcorn and snacks and plush, comfortable seating. And if you're looking for something grandparents and grandkids can enjoy together, IMAX™ is at the top of the list.

To avoid disappointment when bringing a brood, reserve your tickets by phoning in advance. Birthday parties can be arranged.

Getting There

- By car, take 9th Ave. east to Macleod Trail and turn north. Turn west onto 4th Ave., proceeding to 2nd St. Take 2nd St. north to 2nd Ave. The Eau Claire Market is ahead of you, on your right. Pay parking at Eau Claire Market or in the area. About eight minutes from the Calgary Tower.
- By public transit, take CT bus 31 (downtown shuttle) at 7th Ave. and 1st St., across 7th Ave. from the Hudson's Bay store. Get off the bus at 2nd Ave. and 4th St. S.W. and walk east two blocks to 2nd Ave. and 2nd St.
- By bike or on foot, turn west on 9th Ave. to 2nd St. and go north. The market is at the corner of 2nd Ave. and 2nd St.

Nearby

- Eau Claire water park, Eau Claire YMCA, Prince's Island Park. Kid-friendly restaurants abound in this area, from the food fair at Eau Claire Market to Kelsey's and Out West to The Old Spaghetti Factory.

Comment

- There is a first aid kit, but not trained personnel. Telephones at the Eau Claire Market.

Other Theatres

The Calgary Young People's Theatre

204 - 16TH AVE. N.W.
(403) 230-2664
CALGARY
WWW.CADVISION.COM/CYPT

Calgary Young People's Theatre (CYPT) is an established company that presents a season of three productions each year, featuring a cast of teenagers and kids. In addition to shows mounted at Halloween, the Christmas season and Spring break (past productions have included *Alice in Wonderland*, *Charlotte's Web* and *The Secret Garden*), CYPT offers drama classes and summer drama camps as well as a storytelling troupe that visits schools throughout the year.

Please call or check out CYPT's Web site for details of upcoming productions and classes, including venues and costs.

Quest Theatre

310 - 815 - 1ST ST. S.W.
CALGARY
(403) 264-8575

Primarily a touring company, Quest Theatre has been engaging schoolchildren throughout the province for many years. Each of its touring shows also gets a limited run in Mount Royal College's 200-seat Nickle Theatre. The company devotes itself to producing innovative and entertaining works, by both new and established playwrights, that also edify young people. Some of the themes Quest has tackled over the years have included literacy, poverty, conflict resolution and gambling. Even so, a Quest production is never dull or preachy. The company also offers summer day camps out of the Currie Barracks in July. Call for a schedule and to reserve tickets.

☞ Public performances: Fall and Spring, Sat–Sun, 1 pm and 3 pm.

☞ Adults $10, children $7. Discounts available for groups of five or more.

☞ By car, take 9th Ave. east to 1st St. S.E. and turn south. Turn west at 17th Ave. and proceed to 37th St. Turn south on 37th and east on Richard Rd. At the T-intersection, turn south again and follow the signs for the West Entrance at Mount Royal College. Park in the public lot ($1.50 per hour). Walk through the West Entrance and look for the signs pointing you to the Nickle Theatre.
By public transit, take CT bus 13 (Mount Royal) from 8th Ave. and 1st St. S.W. to the college and get off at the West Entrance stop.
By bike, use the car directions.

The Southern Alberta Jubilee Auditorium

1415 - 14TH AVE. N.W.
CALGARY
(403) 297-8000

The Jubilee, located near SAIT, plays host to all kinds of productions and functions, from the annual Kiwanis Festival to shows by the Alberta Ballet to bus-and-truck productions of musicals such as *The Wizard of Oz*. Keep your eyes peeled for performances by the Royal Winnipeg and National Ballets and concerts of all kinds. Travelling *Sesame Street* shows, major children's performers, *The Magic School Bus* live production . . . all are Jubilee fare.

Budget extra time (and a few dollars) for parking beforehand and for getting out of parking lots afterward when you're attending something at the auditorium. Take a little extra money for a drink or snack at intermission.

☞ Year-round: Matinees and evening performances, depending on the company.

☞ Varies depending on the show, from $10 to $80.

☞ By car, take 9th Ave. east to Centre St. and turn north. Turn west onto 4th Ave. and continue west to 10th St. Turn north on 10th, then west onto Kensington Rd. Drive west to 14th St., then turn north. The Jubilee is at the top of the hill on your right. Turn east, then south, to get to the main parking lot. About 15 minutes from the Calgary Tower.
By public transit, take CT bus 10 (Market Mall) from 6th Ave. and 2nd St. S.W. and ride it to 14th St. and 14th Ave. N.W. Or, take the Brentwood train from 7th Ave. and 1st St. S.W. to the SAIT/Jubilee Station.

Stage West

727 - 42ND AVE. S.E.
CALGARY
(403) 243-6642
WWW.STAGEWESTCALGARY.COM

Stage West Dinner Theatre has been serving up theatre and food to largely appreciative adult audiences for many years. Though the shows aren't exactly Stratford Festival quality, the combination of dining and comedy tends to make for a festive evening out. Some dinner shows, like *My Fair Lady*, are suitable for young audiences; others are not. But children, too, appreciate the gala aspect of combining a meal with a theatrical production, so Stage West offers children's matinees three or four times a year. These presentations tend to be cheerful plays on fairy-tale or fanciful themes. The food consists of a buffet featuring foods kids love—such as hot dogs, pizza and ice cream. Children eat first, then watch the show by local company Shadow Productions. The doors open at 11:30 am, the buffet runs from 11:30 am to 12:45 pm, and the show begins at 1 pm.

☞ Three to four Saturday afternoons per year. Call Stage West for exact dates.

☞ Adults $18, children (4 to 12) $15.

☞ By car, take 9th Ave. east to 1st St. S.E. Drive south (1st St. becomes Macleod Trail) to 42nd Ave. Turn east on 42nd and drive to Blackfoot Trail. Continue east past a set of lights, then watch for the Shell gas station on your right; Stage West is behind it.
By public transit, take the Anderson train southbound from Centre St. and 7th Ave. to the 39th Ave. Station and walk south to 42nd Ave. and 7th St. S.E.

Alberta Theatre Projects

Arts Centre
220 - 9th Ave. S.E.
Calgary
(403) 294-7402
www.atplive.com

Alberta Theatre Projects (ATP) is one of the "braver" theatre companies in town. Although it occasionally mounts a family-friendly production such as *My Fair Lady*, the company is more likely to tackle edgier stuff. So make sure to do your research before splurging on a fun-filled night with the kids at the theatre. Call ATP in advance and ask about the appropriateness of the material you're considering—just because the word "Christmas" appears in the title, don't assume it's a heartwarming story—and give voice to any special concerns you might have, about profanity, nudity or even the use of a strobe light. Playrites is a fabulous festival that takes place in January and February every year, featuring readings as well as performances. Again, call ahead and check the material out before taking the kids.

☞ Year-round. Call for showtimes.

☞ Regular shows: Between $20 and $41.
Playrite shows: Between $14 and $24.

☞ The Arts Centre is two blocks east of the Calgary Tower.

Chapter 7

Animals, Farms & Zoos

Introduction

Calgary may be a metropolitan city, but the land around it remains horse and cattle country. Stay at a guest ranch and your family can experience the lifestyle led by the first settlers to the area. Learn how to care for livestock, attend a local rodeo and participate in a cattle drive—or simply saddle up and roam through thousands of hectares of scenic land. Plenty of local outfitters and ranchers also offer trail rides from one-hour tours to week-long pack trips into the mountains. For a different kind of riding experience, head to Spruce Meadows, a world-famous show jumping facility just outside Calgary.

For another taste of rural life, visit a working farm. During several months of the year, the sweet taste of summer is as close as the nearest "U-pick" farm. Animals, big and small, are always a hit and at Butterfield Acres little ones can cuddle up to rabbits, feed the donkeys and see more exotic species, too. And for youngsters keen on birds, the Inglewood Bird Sanctuary offers the opportunity to watch feathered friends in their natural habitat.

Happy Trails!

NOTE

Kids will also see all sorts of animals at:
The Calgary Zoo (Chapter 1, page 21)

Hands-on Farm Fun at BUTTERFIELD ACRES CHILDREN'S FARM

OFF ROCKY RIDGE RD. N.W.
CALAGARY
(403) 239-0638

Butterfield Acres offers city slickers the chance to experience life on a working farm: kids can milk a goat, ride a pony or take a tractor-pulled tour of the back pasture. They're also welcome to pet the horses, donkeys, calves and other animals, cuddle the rabbits or scamper across the troll's bridge with the goats. Spring is the perfect time to visit—from fluffy chicks to lively lambs; new life infuses the farm. Keep your eyes peeled, as you just might catch a glimpse of a mom giving birth to a calf or a foal.

Kids with inquiring minds can examine the saddlery in the tack house or look at different kinds of animal feed and grain in the grain house. Throughout the farm, signs offer information about animals and their habits. Youngsters with a taste for the exotic won't be disappointed

☞ SEASONS AND TIMES
➛ Summer: Daily, 10 am–4 pm.
Spring and Fall: Weekends, 10 am–4 pm.

☞ COST
➛ Adults $6.75, seniors and children (under 19) $4.75.
Season's passes available. Credit cards accepted.

☞ GETTING THERE
➛ By car, take Centre St. north to 6th Ave. S.W. (its name changes to Bow Trail) and go west. Turn north on Crowchild Trail and continue on until Rocky Ridge Rd. N.W. Head north for approximately three kilometres to the farm. Free parking on site. About 30 minutes from the Calgary Tower.

☞ COMMENT
➛ Parts of the farm are not accessible to wheelchairs or strollers. Plan a 2-hour visit.

either. Butterfield Acres is home to shaggy highland cattle, emus, llamas, alpacas and a Falabella miniature horse.

Feeding the animals is always a popular activity, and livestock feed is available at the main gate. If your brood starts to get hungry, head to the treed eating area for a picnic. A duck pond and playground are nearby. Week-long summer camps will teach kids ages 3 to 12 about a different farm animal each day. Birthday parties can be arranged.

Jump Right in at SPRUCE MEADOWS

Off Hwy. AY 22X
Calgary
(403) 974-4200
WWW.SPRUCEMEADOWS.COM

Originally the hobby farm of a local businessman, Spruce Meadows has become one of the globe's top venues for the sport of show jumping. Four major outdoor tournaments, featuring some of the best horses and riders, are held each summer and the action both inside and outside the immaculate grass rings will delight children of all ages. In addition to the jumping competitions, visitors may have the opportunity of witnessing the RCMP's

Seasons and Times

➛ Year-round: Daily, 10 am—6 pm. Extended hours during tournaments, call ahead for details.

Cost

➛ Tournaments: Adults $5, seniors and children (12 and under) free. Admission is free when competitions are not in progress.

Musical Ride, watching precision quadrille dressage exercises or seeing amazing displays of stunt riding or skydiving. During the Masters tournament, there's also the popular Battle of the Breeds competition. Events such as precision driving, barrel racing and jeopardy jumping highlight the versatility of Alberta's horse breeds

☞ GETTING THERE

➛ By car, take 9th Ave. east to 1st St. S.E. (its name changes to Macleod Trail) and go south to the edge of the city. Turn west on Hwy. 22 X and follow the signs to the Meadows. Free parking on site. About 35 minutes from the Calgary Tower.

➛ By public transit, during tournaments a shuttle bus takes visitors to and from the Anderson LRT station.

☞ COMMENT

➛ First aid and meal service are only available during tournaments.

When youngsters begin to fidget, join the activity in the Plaza. Sample crêpes and other international delicacies, thrill to the sounds of a marching band or watch the Spruce Meadows Prairie Dogs as they race over, under and through obstacles. There are also pony rides, singers, dancers, face-painters, horse-drawn wagon rides and other attractions. If your children have any energy left, head to the park, where a replica carriage and tire swings inspire even more adventures.

Though the tournaments are the main draw, Spruce Meadows is open to the public when competitions are not scheduled. Then, children can wander through the barns or watch horses and riders practice jumping.

Flock to INGLEWOOD BIRD SANCTUARY

2425 - 9th Ave. S.E.
Calgary
(403) 269-6688

At the Inglewood Bird Sanctuary, kids will not only learn about birds, they'll also get the opportunity to spot some in the wild. Over 2.5 kilometres of stroller-friendly trails take birdwatchers through riverine forest, along the Bow River and around a quiet lagoon. Benches placed at regular intervals offer visitors a peaceful spot from which to watch. There's a lot to see. Over 270 bird species, including great-horned owls, bald eagles, ring-necked pheasants and red-winged blackbirds, have been observed within this 32-hectare refuge.

When the kids get tired of walking, head to the interpretive centre, which houses a small number of interesting exhibits. Here, they can learn about bird migration, open a series of colourful doors to view the nests and eggs of different species or match various nesting holes to the appropriate bird. They can also report their bird sightings to sanctuary staff—any rare or special species will be noted on a bulletin board.

☞ Seasons and Times

➛ Summer: Mon—Thu, 9 am—8 pm; Fri—Sun, 9 am—5 pm.
Winter: Tue—Sun, 10 am—4 pm.

☞ Cost

➛ Free. Donations accepted.

☞ Getting There

➛ By car, take 9th Ave. east to Sanctuary Rd. and turn south. Free parking on site. About 15 minutes from the Calgary Tower.

☞ Comment

➛ Visitors are not permitted to feed the birds. Plan a 2-hour visit.

P

Inglewood runs a variety of nature-related courses for children and families, such as birdhouse construction and animal track discovery. Youngsters can also explore the world of birds, insects, mammals and plants at camps held during spring break and over the summer.

Discover the Old West
STAY AT A GUEST RANCH

Cowboys, cattle and horses—if your children are fascinated by tales of the old west, why not let them experience life on a real working ranch? A number of scenic guest ranches in the Calgary area welcome visitors. And while your family will not be required to participate in the running of the operation, most kids love to help out with such chores as fencing, checking on the horses and cows, and feeding and grooming the livestock.

> **Seasons and Times**
> ➛ Varies, but generally May—Oct. Reservations required.
>
> **Cost**
> ➛ Varies. Expect to pay at least $170 to $200 per person per night based on double occupancy. Prices may be higher during peak season (mid-June to mid-September) and generally include riding, all meals, snacks, accommodations and activities.

Trail riding, fishing and hiking are other popular activities and some ranches offer wagon rides, hayrides, western entertainers, native ceremonies, lasso contests, riding lessons, chuckwagon rides and cattle drives. Saddle-weary parents will appreciate a soak in the hot tub at the end of the day. You may also have the opportunity to attend community dances, dinners and rodeos. Other ranches don't offer much in the way of activities, they prefer to leave you to your own devices in the peace and solitude of the country.

Accommodations vary as well; you might have a private room with attached bathroom in the ranch house, or you might stay in your own rustic log cabin. For the more adventurous, there is sometimes the option of sleeping in a teepee. Getting to know everyone is easy; at the majority of the ranches your family will eat with the hosts and staff in a large kitchen.

Bar C Canadian Adventure Resort
Cochrane
(403) 932-2665 or 1-887-932-BARC
www.bar-c.com

Highland View Guest Ranch
High River
(403) 395-2246

Homeplace Ranch
Priddis
(403) 931-3245 or 1-887-931-3245

Lynnwood Ranch
Okotoks
(403) 938-2203

Willowbrook Ranch
Millarville
(403) 933-5448

Indulge Yourself PLACES TO PICK YOUR OWN PRODUCE

Plump sweet berries, crisp lettuce, tender peas . . . produce that's straight from the garden can be a real treat. If you don't have a garden of your own (or it's just not as big as you would like), your family can still indulge when you take them to one of several "U-pick" farms around Calgary. Pack a picnic lunch, bring along hats and sunscreen for everyone and spend a few happy hours harvesting in the fields. Then enjoy!

Some of the farms listed below offer everything from berries and vegetables to herbs and flowers. Others only have berries. Whatever you choose, be sure to call before you visit—the availability of most crops will vary with the year's growing conditions. Also, facilities vary from farm to farm. Some provide visitors with picnic tables, toilets and small cafés, and may sell homemade pies, jams, jellies and other delicacies. At others you'll only find fields and fields of produce to pick. Call ahead to get directions.

FRAY'S BERRY FARM
BOUNDARY RD.
(403) 936-5413

CROPS INCLUDE JUNE-BEARING STRAWBERRIES (JULY AND AUGUST), STRAWBERRIES, RASPBERRIES AND SASKATOONS (MID-JULY TO AUGUST). THERE ARE TOILETS AND PICNIC TABLES ON SITE.

Premium Organic Farms
(403) 203-1095

Mixed vegetables and organic produce are available.

The Garden
(403) 936-5569

Crops include June-bearing strawberries (July and August), day-neutral strawberries (August to September), raspberries, peas, carrots, mixed vegetables, herbs and fresh and dry flowers. There's also a pond stocked with rainbow trout and garden plots are available to rent.

The Saskatoon Farm
(403) 938-6245

Saskatoon berries. There are picnic tables and an on-site café that serves up saskatoon pie and coffee. Homemade pies, syrups, jams and buffalo sausage are also available at the café. Bedding plants, perennials, trees and shrubs are for sale at the farm's greenhouse.

Yeehaw! SADDLE UP FOR A TRAIL RIDE

Splash through clear mountain streams, cross an old Indian trail, circle a flowering alpine meadow—trail riding allows children to see Alberta's foothills and mountains as the first pioneers did, on horseback. From one-hour rides to pack trips lasting five days or longer, a number of ranches and stables in the Calgary area are waiting to give your family a truly western experience.

Riders of all skill levels can be accommodated and, though most trips are suitable for the over-five crowd, some stables do offer pony lead-arounds for younger children (about $10 for 30 minutes). Birthday party packages, wagon and sleigh rides, and summer day camps are sometimes available as well. Children eight or older can learn basic riding skills, safety and how to care for a horse and its equipment.

Pack trips can be combined with other adventures such as whitewater rafting or a stay at a guest ranch. Shorter morning or afternoon rides may include pancake breakfasts or steak dinners. Expect to pay at least $40 per person for a two-hour ride and $90 per person for an all-day ride. Kids' prices are often slightly cheaper. For pack trips, expect to pay at least $165 per person for a two-day trip. Longer and combination trips will be more expensive and generally include accommodations, food, cooks, horses, guides and wranglers.

Riding helmets are provided at some operations. For maximum comfort, wear jeans, a hat and runners, cowboy boots or shoes with a sturdy, defined heel. Bring a warm sweater or jacket. On longer trips, be prepared to bring your own ground sheet, sleeping bag, rain gear, riding boots, warm clothing and personal gear.

☞ **Seasons and Times**

➛ Varies, but generally May—Sept. Some stables are open year-round. Reservations are required for pack trips and may be required for shorter rides.

Anchor D Guiding and Outfitting

Black Diamond
(403) 933-2867
www.anchord.com

Griffin Valley Ranch
Cochrane
(403) 932-7433

Happy Trails Riding Stables
Calgary
(403) 251-3344

M&M Ranch
Bragg Creek
(403) 949-3272

Rafter Six Ranch
Seebe
(403) 264-1251 or 1-888-267-2624

Saddle Peak Trail Rides
Cochrane
(403) 932-3299

Chapter 8

green spaces

Introduction

Calgary is well served by its almost 6,600 hectares of parks. Scattered over 2,700 locations, they offer a vast array of outdoor experiences. There are open city spaces such as River Park where dogs can run free alongside their romping owners; sheltered spots such as Sandy Beach with barbecue pits for roasting marshmallows in milder weather; and bits of wild, tangled, waterside forest including the Weaselhead end of Glenmore Park, ideal for walks or bike rides.

Riley Park has a splendid playground and a free wading pool, which appeals to older and younger children, with massive trees providing shade from Calgary's brilliant sunshine. Tromping the trails of Nose Hill Park will yield interesting finds to young botanists and birdwatchers. Fish Creek's long, hilly pathways invite bicyclists, strollers, picnickers and horseback riders, and chances there are good of seeing deer, beavers, hawks and owls.

For general information about City of Calgary parks, call the City of Calgary's Parks and Recreation Playline at (403) 268-2300. Whenever you head for a park, pack snacks, drinks and warm clothes so a pleasant excursion doesn't have to be abbreviated. Find out where the washrooms (if any) are at the start of your jaunt to prevent "accidents" later on (most city park washrooms are open from May until late September), and unless it's noted, assume there are no diaper-changing facilities.

Untamed Wilderness FISH CREEK PROVINCIAL PARK

15979 Bow Bottom Trail S.E. (Visitor Centre)
Calgary
(403) 297-5293
www.gov.ab.ca/env/parks/prov_parks/fishcreek

This massive tract of land, one of Canada's largest urban parks, encompasses 1,189 hectares of rocky escarpment, grassy valley, towering pines and rushing creek. A Natural Heritage Site, Fish Creek Park welcomes all manner of outdoor enthusiasts. It's also home to white-tailed deer, coyotes, peregrine falcons and great horned owls, as well as other animals.

Start your first trip to the park at the Visitor Centre, which has interpretive displays that outline the history of Fish Creek valley. The centre also stocks maps so you can enjoy the park to the fullest. Pre-programmed Adventure Packs are available to help families explore a variety of topics, or attend one of the park's interpretive events. There are 13 day-use areas at Fish Creek, including the popular beach at Sikome Lake and the barbecue pits at Bebo Grove (take your own firewood). At the Shannon Terrace day-use area, a stable (Horsin Around, 238-6665) offers pony rides,

☞ Seasons and Times

➛ Park: Year-round, generally, 8 am–11 pm in summer and 8 am–6 pm in winter. Call the number above for details.
Visitor Centre: Year-round, Mon–Fri, 8:15 am– noon and 1 pm–4:30 pm; Sat–Sun, 10 am–4 pm. Closed on statutory holidays.

☞ Cost

➛ Park: Free. Fees may apply for certain activities.
Horsin Around: Pony rides (15 minutes) $5, trail rides (90 minutes) $25, hayrides and sleigh rides (reservations required, prices vary).

☞ Getting There

➛ By car, take 9th Ave. east to 1st St. S.E. and turn south (it turns into Macleod Trail). Continue along Macleod Trail to Canyon Meadows Dr., then turn east and follow Canyon Meadows to Bow Bottom Trail. Turn south and follow the signs to the Bow Valley Ranch Visitor Centre. Free parking on site. About 20 minutes from the Calgary Tower. Other major access routes include Canyon Meadows Dr., Macleod Trail, Elbow Dr., 24th St. S.W. and 37th St. S.W. Parking areas are scattered throughout the park.

➛ By public transit, take the southbound LRT from 7th Ave. S.E. to Anderson Station, transfer to CT bus 83 and ride it to Sikome Lake. For bus routes to other parts of the park, call Calgary Transit at 262-1000.

☞ Nearby

➛ Southland Leisure Centre, Ton o' Fun.

☞ Comment

➛ Pick a part of the park to explore and then plan accordingly. Partially accessible for wheelchairs and strollers. Plan at least a 2-hour visit.

trail rides, hayrides and sleigh rides. A hill near Sikome Lake is a favourite with tobogganers.

In addition to the natural experience on offer here, there's a decidedly civilized spot for a rest and a snack, or a meal: Annie Bannister's Café (225-3920) is located in an historic house near the Visitor Centre.

Fish Creek Environmental Learning Centre (297-7827) caters to 18,000 school children annually with special programs. So does Bow Valley Ranch Visitor Centre (297-5293).

Learning about Wetlands
ELBOW VALLEY CONSTRUCTED WETLAND

Hwy. 8 (Glenmore Trail)
Calgary
(403) 221-4660

One of Calgary's newest and lesser-known parks, this Elbow Valley destination was the first wetland constructed in the city. It's designed to educate visitors on storm water management and wetland habitats, and also makes for a pleasant, short walk that's well suited to young children who tire easily. A series of bridges and boardwalks links the different sections of the wetland, and there are interpretive signs that are easy to understand. Bring your binoculars and field guides and watch for birds, such as the spotted sandpiper, red-winged blackbird and red-tipped hawk. You can also inspect the water for all kinds of bugs. Please don't bring dip nets or buckets, though. There are no facilities here, so pack

☞ Seasons and Times

→ Year-round: Daily, dawn—dusk.

☞ Cost

→ Free.

☞ Getting There

→ Take Centre St. north to 2nd Ave., then turn west and head for Bow Trail. Take Bow Trail west to 37th St. Turn south onto 37th and proceed to Glenmore Trail (Hwy. 8). Follow Glenmore Trail west 800 metres past the intersection with Sarcee Trail. The wetland is on your left. Free parking on site. About 15 minutes from the Calgary Tower.

☞ Nearby

→ North Glenmore Park.

☞ Comment

→ Plan a 30-minute visit.

snacks and drinks before you leave, and make sure everyone is wearing bug repellent.

Leafy Glades
EDWORTHY PARK AND DOUGLAS FIR TRAIL

45TH ST. S.W. TO SPRUCE DR.
CALGARY
(403) 221-4560

Time seems to stand still on a sunny afternoon in a park like Edworthy, though children are anything but static. The park snuggles up to city trails for in-line skating, biking or walking a stroller. Edworthy itself offers sheltered and open picnic tables, barbecue pits, a playground, hiking and cross-country ski trails. There's even canoe access to the Bow River, although no swimming. A young fly fisherman could do worse than to settle down on the banks of the river and cast to his or her heart's content (watch river levels for safety).

Lowery Gardens Natural Area is another enticement here, as is the Douglas Fir Trail, which winds uphill from Edworthy and offers a good

> ☞ **SEASONS AND TIMES**
> → Year-round: Dawn—dusk.
>
> ☞ **COST**
> → Free.
>
> ☞ **GETTING THERE**
> → By car, take Centre St. north to 2nd Ave. and turn west. Follow 2nd Ave. to Bow Trail and continue west on Bow Trail until 45th St. Then turn north. Drive until just after 45th meets Spruce Dr. Free parking on site. About 15 minutes from the Calgary Tower.
> → By public transit, take CT bus 1 (Bowness) to the park.

cardio workout for parent and child alike. It would be difficult for a wheelchair or stroller to manage the trail.

NEARBY

- Shouldice Park, Wildwood Arts Centre.

COMMENT

- Partially wheelchair and stroller accessible. Plan a 2-hour visit.

Active Excursions
NORTH GLENMORE PARK

37TH ST. AT 66TH AVE. S.W.
CALGARY
(403) 221-3550

On fine-weather evenings and weekends, North Glenmore Park is as busy as can be. In-line skaters, bicyclists, picnickers, walkers and sailors pack the park, which overlooks the Glenmore Reservoir. At one end is the Glenmore Canoe and Rowing Club House (246-5757) and its boat dock. At the other is Weaselhead "Flats," a hilly natural area that takes walkers and bikers down to the

SEASONS AND TIMES

- Year-round: Daily, 6 am—11 pm.

COST

- Free.

GETTING THERE

- By car, take 9th Ave. east to 1st St. S.E. Drive south on 1st to 17th Ave. and turn west. Continue going west on 17th until 37th St., then turn south following 37th to where it meets 66th Ave. The parking lot for North Glenmore Park is on your right. About 15 minutes from the Calgary Tower.
- By public transit, take the southbound LRT train to Chinook Station, then transfer to CT bus 47 (Lakeview) and ride it to the park.
- By bicycle, use the car directions.

☞ **NEARBY**
➛ Elbow Valley Constructed Wetland, South Glenmore Park.

☞ **COMMENT**
➛ Parts of the park are not wheelchair or stroller accessible; Weaselhead has a pretty steep hill. Plan at least a 1-hour visit.

water's edge. In between are barbecue pits, picnic tables, park benches, playgrounds, and lots of grassy space for pick-up games of practically anything. You can hike here, cross-country ski, host a gigantic family picnic, play tennis or launch your canoe. Hot air balloons often drift overhead; some even start out from the park. With the reservoir glittering below the escarpment and happy fellow outdoors enthusiasts bustling by you on the paths, this is one family outing that could become a favourite.

Take insect repellent with you in the summer, especially if you plan to walk into Weaselhead. And pack snacks and drinks; there's nothing on site.

Urban Unwinding at RILEY PARK

800 - 12TH ST. N.W.
CALGARY
(403) 221-3955

☞ **SEASONS AND TIMES**
➛ Year-round: Daily, 7 am—11 pm.

☞ **COST**
➛ Free.

This verdant section of Louise Crossing, better known as Kensington, is a joy to visit in the summer months and pleasant in the other seasons as well. Pull the kids around on a sled when it's snowy, or take them to the big, beautiful playground in spring or fall. In the summer, though, there's the added attraction of the free wading pool, which is surrounded by big, sweeping trees. A kiosk in the pool area sells snacks then, too.

On Wednesday afternoons during the summer and early fall, the Hillhurst-Sunnyside Farmers' Market takes place at the community centre across the street from the park, beginning at 3:30 pm. Snacks—fresh fruit, bread and sweets—can be purchased there and taken back to the picnic tables at Riley, or you can bring food from home and use the barbecue pits. In fact, an entire afternoon can easily be whiled away here.

☞ **GETTING THERE**

➛ By car, take Centre St. north, turn west onto 4th Ave. continuing on until it meets 10th St. Turn north onto 10th, then west onto 5th Ave. N.W. Follow 5th to 12th St. Find free parking on a side street but watch the signs for restrictions.

➛ By public transit, take CT bus 4 (Northaven) and ride it to the park.

➛ By bicycle, use the car directions.

☞ **NEARBY**

➛ Jubilee Auditorium, Peters Drive-in, Prince's Island, Calgary Zoo.

☞ **COMMENT**

➛ Partial wheelchair access. Plan a 2-hour visit in the summer, 30 minutes in the winter.

Hidden Oasis
DEVONIAN GARDENS

317 - 7TH AVE. S.W.
CALGARY
(403) 268-5207

You wouldn't guess it by looking at Calgary's concrete and steel skyline, but in the middle of downtown lies a restful oasis. Devonian Gardens, located on the top level of the Toronto Dominion Square building and measuring about a hectare, is the largest indoor garden in Alberta. Foliage isn't all this garden offers. Younger children, especially, get a charge out of Devonian's flower-lined walkways, splashing fountains, statues and pools full of pudgy rainbow trout and koi. For $1, they can buy some fish food on site, sprinkle it over the water's surface and cause a small but fascinating flurry of activity.

At the east end of Devonian Gardens is an indoor playground. Your group may also stumble onto an interesting festivity of one sort or another,

☞ SEASONS AND TIMES
➛Year-round: Daily, 9 am—9 pm.

☞ COST
➛ Free. (Donation of $1 per person welcomed.)

☞ GETTING THERE
➛ By car, take Centre St. north and turn west on 6th Ave. Turn south on Barclay Mall (3rd St.) S.W., then park at a meter or lot nearby as parking on the Stephen Avenue Mall is unlikely. About five minutes from the Calgary Tower.
➛ By public transit, take the westbound LRT along 7th Ave. to 4th St. S.W. and walk one block east. TD Square is on the corner of 7th Ave. and 3rd St. CT bus 1 stops at 7th Ave. and 4th St. also.
➛ By bicycle, turn west on 9th Ave. and north on Barclay (3rd St).

☞ COMMENT
➛ No diaper-changing facilities. Food kiosks on the lower level of TD Square and in Eaton Centre and Scotia Centre next to it. Outside of business hours, access the gardens via the 8th Ave. or 7th Ave. glass elevators. Plan a 1-hour visit.

as this is a popular place for weddings, photo shoots (permits required) and fashion shows. There are often free concerts and other performances at noon, and art shows are presented too.

Devonian Gardens is an especially fine escape from the confines of home in the wintertime. When it's 30 below outside, scampering through a warm, humid garden and then retreating to a park bench for a picnic is a sure cure for boredom. Birthday parties can be booked here; the charge is $32 for the first hour, $19 for each hour following.

Fun for All Seasons
BOWNESS PARK

8900 - 48th Ave. N.W.
Calgary
(403) 221-3955

A lovely green space in the city's northwest, Bowness Park is easily overlooked by people who rarely venture into this area. They don't know what they're missing. In the winter, Bowness is a snowy wonderland where skating along the tree-lined lagoon at nighttime, under bridges and around bonfires, is a truly memorable event. Cross-country skiing offers pleasant vistas.

Seasons and Times

➛ Year-round: Daily, 7 am—10 pm.

Cost

➛ Park: Free.
Pedal boats (two and four-person, 30 minutes): $6 and $10.
Canoes (30 minutes): $6. Life jackets are included.
Deposit of ID required. An adult must accompany small children.
Minigolf: $4 per person.
Riverside Playland: Rates vary, call 286-9889.

☞ **GETTING THERE**

➛ By car, take Centre St. north to 16th Ave. and turn west. Continue along 16th Ave. (it then becomes the Trans-Canada Hwy.) until you see Canada Olympic Park on your left. Turn north onto Bowfort Rd. and follow it until it turns into 83rd St. Turn west onto Bowness Rd. (which becomes 85th St.). Follow the signs to the park, which will be on your left. Free parking on site. About 20 minutes from the Calgary Tower.

➛ By public transit, take CT bus 1 (Bowness) and ride it to the park.

☞ **COMMENT**

➛ Diaper-changing facilities. Plan at least a 2-hour visit.

In the summer, a stroll along the paths might take your brood to a stand of Douglas firs where a few of the trees are over four centuries old. Rent a canoe or a pedal boat and enjoy a trip around the lagoon and its spectacular fountain; if it's a hot day, investigate the spray and wading pools. Across the Stoney Trail suspension bridge, Riverside Playland has a few fun rides for kids. There's also minigolf and a miniature train. Pony rides are offered year-round, weather permitting (weekends only in the winter). These Riverside temptations will interest those younger than seven more than older children, who may be more keen to bicycle or explore the park's trails. In any case, a good time will be had by all if you spend a few hours here.

Out for a Stroll RIVER PARK AND SANDY BEACH

**OFF 14A ST. BETWEEN 38TH AVE. AND 50TH AVE. S.W.
CALGARY
(403) 221-3550**

River Park is a wide-open plain, perfect for kids and dogs. Children will have plenty to see here as they run around, fly kites, throw balls, or walk along the edge of the park's cliff with its view of the Elbow River below and the city skyline to the north.

Down the hill at the south end of River Park is lovely, sheltered Sandy Beach, which contains a playground, a bike path that's accessible to strollers, and barbecue pits. Sandy Beach may be its name, but the "beach," really a clearing on one side of the river, is more rocky than sandy. Nevertheless, when the Elbow isn't running too fast, waders with watchful parents can wander in a few feet. Cross the bridge past the beach and take either

☞ SEASONS AND TIMES

➛Year-round: Daily, 6 am—11 pm.

☞ COST

➛ Free.

☞ GETTING THERE

➛ By car, take 1st St. S.E. south to 17th Ave. and turn west. At 14th St. turn south and drive up the hill. Follow 14th St. to its end and then turn west onto 38th Ave. Turn south onto 14A St. River Park is on your left and stretches to 50th Ave. On 50th, turn east and head down the gravel path to get to Sandy Beach. For River Park, park on the street or in the parking lot just to the east of 50th. There is parking in a free lot down the gravel road at Sandy Beach. About 15 minutes from the Calgary Tower.

➛ By public transit, take CT bus 13 (Mount Royal) to the park. To get to Sandy Beach, get off at 50th Ave. and 16th St. and walk down the gravel road. To get to the north end of River Park, get off the bus at 38th Ave. and 14A St.

➛ By bicycle, use the car directions.

the meandering, rougher path through the forest or the paved path by the field and you'll come to Riverdale Avenue in Elbow Park. One of the city's more attractive neighbourhoods, it's a place with quiet, shady streets and people who don't seem to mind lollygaggers trooping past ogling their discreet mansions.

Take sweaters or jackets. Sandy Beach is shady and can get cool. And bring snacks and drinks. Sandy Beach offers all the amenities that are listed on page 165. River Park has no accoutrements.

COMMENT

→ Wheelchairs may have difficulty at River Park. Group picnics at Sandy Beach by permit. Plan at least a 1-hour visit.

Other Green Spaces

Nose Hill Park Natural Area

OFF 14TH ST. BETWEEN JOHN LAURIE BLVD. AND BERKSHIRE BLVD. N.W.
CALGARY
(403) 221-3955
WWW.GOV.CALGARY.AB.CA

Perched high above the city and offering panoramic views, Nose Hill Park is an ideal untamed spot for a gambol with children and dogs (it's an off-leash area). Like Fish Creek Park, this space is enormous, encompassing 1,128 hectares of uncultivated grassland, the largest area of natural prairie in the city. The hill's big boulders are glacial erratics, vestiges of glacial retreat after the last Ice Age.

Nose Hill is a grand place to fly a kite or take a hike, and in wintertime it's a marvellous place to go tobogganing. Among its natural attractions is the communal roosting of crows that takes place in the late afternoons and early evenings from March through early October. Vegetation on the hill has been influenced by the crows, which gather in the thousands and drop seeds gathered from all over the city onto the ground beneath them. Dress warmly as it gets breezy at this park.

☞ Year-round: Daily, 7 am–11 pm.

☞ Free.

☞ By car, take Centre St. north to 16th Ave. and turn west. Turn north onto 14th St. and drive to John Laurie Blvd. Nose Hill is directly in front of you. Free parking on site. About 20 minutes from the Calgary Tower.
By public transit, take CT bus 4 (Northhaven) and walk to the park off 14th St.

Richmond Green

33RD AVE. AND 25TH ST. S.W.
CALGARY
(403) 221-3530
WWW.GOV.CALGARY.AB.CA

This bowl of green space at the confluence of Crowchild Trail and Richmond Road never seems to be crowded, despite being blessed with a playground, tennis courts and bright southwest exposure. In the winter, it offers a fine tobogganing hill behind the Carewest building, with a steeper incline in the middle and a more relaxed one at either side.

☞ Park: Year-round, daily, 7 am–11 pm.
Tennis courts: May–Oct (weather dependent), Mon–Fri, 11 am–2 pm and 5 pm–8:30 pm; Sat–Sun, 9 am–8:30 pm.

☞ Park: Free.
Tennis courts: $4 per court per hour. During off hours, the courts are free.

☞ Take Centre St. north to 6th Ave. and drive west until 6th merges with Bow Trail. Take the Crowchild Trail south exit and drive south; take the Richmond Rd. W. exit off Crowchild. Continue along Richmond Rd. and turn south onto Sarcee Rd. Take a left at the Carewest sign on the left, before the road's first corner. Park in the lot. About 15 minutes from the Calgary Tower.
By public transit, take CT buses 111, 108, 112 or 18 (Lakeview).
By bicycle, take 9th Ave. east, turn south onto 1st St. S.E. Turn west onto 17th Ave. and south onto 37th St. At the corner of Richmond Rd. (33rd Ave.) turn east and ride to Sarcee Rd. Turn south onto Sarcee and look for the Carewest sign on your left.

Stanley Park

42ND AVE. AND 1A ST. S.W.
CALGARY
(403) 221-3530
WWW.GOV.CALGARY.AB.CA

An outdoor swimming pool, coin-operated tennis nets, a playground, picnic tables, barbecue pits and canoe launch access make Stanley Park a real family destination during the summer, from June 28 to September 6. Its proximity to a lovely trail along the Elbow River means it's also worth visiting during the mild days of winter, when the pool is closed but a few die-hard ducks may still frolic by the water's edge. Toilets and water fountains operate during summer only. You can fish here. The park is partially accessible to wheelchairs and strollers.

☞ Year-round: Daily, 7 am–11 pm.
Swimming pool: Early June–late June, Mon–Fri, 9 am–8 pm; Sat–Sun, 9 am–9 pm. Late June–early Sept, Mon–Fri, 1 pm–8 pm; Sat–Sun, 9 am–9 pm.

☞ Park: Free.
Swimming pool: Adults (18 to 64) $4, seniors (65 and up) and students (7 to 17) $2, children (2 to 6) $1, under 2 free, families $9.

☞ By car, take 9th Ave. east to 1st St. S.E. and turn south continuing until it merges with Macleod Trail. Turn west from Macleod onto 42nd Ave. S.W. and watch for the Stanley Park signs. Free parking on site. About ten minutes from the Calgary Tower.
By public transit, take CT bus 10 (Southcentre) to 42nd Ave. and Macleod Trail and walk two short blocks west.
By bicycle, take 9th Ave. west, turning south onto 5th St. Cross the little bridge and turn right onto Rideau Rd. At the end of the street is a bicycle path. Follow it until you reach Stanley Park on your left.

Pearce Estate Park

17TH AVE. AND 17 A ST. S.E.
CALGARY
(403) 221-3530
WWW.GOV.CALGARY.AB.CA

This charming park cuddles up to the Sam Livingston Fish Hatchery (page 113), so feel free to pop in there for a self-guided tour and see a variety of trout species that are used to stock lakes throughout the province (call 297-6561). Otherwise, enjoy the picnic tables, barbecue stands, playground and disc golf course. Beach volleyball is another option; take your own ball. Amble over the creek to the river's edge to take a look at the weir, an extremely dangerous but fascinating bit of waterworks. For a guided nature walk, call 269-8289. Take your own food and drink, as there's nothing sold on site. Toilets (available from late May through early October) are locked at 4 pm.

☞ Park: Year-round, daily, 5 am—11 pm.
Hatchery: May 1—Sept 30, Mon—Fri, 10 am—4 pm; weekends and holidays, 1 pm—5 pm. Oct 1—Apr 30, Mon—Fri, 10 am—4 pm.

☞ The park and Sam Livingston Fish Hatchery are free.

☞ By car, take 9th Ave. east, which merges with 17th Ave., and then turn north on 17A St. S.E. Free parking on site. About ten minutes from the Calgary Tower.
By public transit, take CT bus 1 (Forest Lawn) to 19th St. and Blackfoot Trail and walk one block north.
By bicycle, use the car directions.

Confederation Park

10TH ST. N. AT 24TH AVE. N.W.
CALGARY
(403) 221-3955
WWW.GOV.CALGARY.AB.CA

For many families it's a tradition to visit Confederation Park at least once a year, over the Christmas holidays. The magnificent displays of lights presented annually by the Lions Club at the 14th Street end of the park invite crowds of onlookers. An evening of tobogganing (at the east end of the park) or cross-country skiing can be capped off by an up-close look at this festive extravaganza.

Confederation Park's wide-open spaces, paved pathways and creek invite sports lovers, cyclists and walkers in the summertime. Tennis courts and a baseball diamond are also on site. The park is partially accessible to wheelchairs and strollers. Toilets are open from May to late September only.

☞ Year-round: Daily, dawn–dusk.
Tennis: May–Oct, daily.
Christmas lights display: December.

☞ Park: Free.
Tennis ($4 per hour): Mon–Fri, 11 am–2 pm and 5 pm–8:30 pm; Sat–Sun and holidays, 9 am–8:30 pm. Other times free.

☞ By car, take Centre St. north to 16th Ave. Turn west and drive to 10th St. Turn north onto 10th and drive to 24th Ave. N.W. Free parking in the lots on 30th Ave. and on 10th St. About 15 minutes from the Calgary Tower.
By public transit, take CT bus 10 (Market Mall) to 20th Ave. and 14th St. Walk north for two blocks, then one block east, or transfer to the 414 shuttle.
By bicycle, use the car directions.

CHAPTER 9

HISTORICAL SITES

Introduction

In the grand scheme of things, Calgary isn't a particularly old city. Founded in 1875 when the North West Mounted Police arrived to bust up whiskey trading and establish a fort at the confluence of the Bow and Elbow rivers, Calgary has long depended on feisty, independent-minded people with a genuine pioneering spirit to define its character.

Affectionately called Cowtown, Calgary's European heritage is largely one of ranchers, farmers and oil speculators, and these aspects of the city's history are celebrated in places such as the Western Heritage Centre, Heritage Park and Fort Calgary. Before the white man ever set foot in North America, however, Indian bands roamed the prairie and foothills of Alberta. The Tsuu T'ina Museum tells the history of one such band. Others—including the Blood, Siksika, Peigan, Stoney and Cree peoples—are celebrated in the First Nations galleries at the Glenbow Museum. Glenbow also pays tribute to the non-natives who helped found Calgary, the city known as "the gateway to the Rockies."

Bits and pieces of Calgary's history can also be found at the other museums listed in this book's Museums chapter. So kindle that pioneering spirit and take your kids on an adventure into the past.

NOTE

For more Historical Sites that welcome children, see chapter 12.

Investigating Cowtown FORT CALGARY HISTORIC PARK

750 - 9TH AVE. S.E.
CALGARY
(403) 290-1875
WWW.FORTCALGARY.AB.CA

Reputedly, Fort Calgary was once a rather dry place with little to see besides the 16-hectare site's interpretive centre, where items celebrating Calgary's heritage were stuck behind glass. No more.

Recently revamped, this revitalized centre now offers a fun-filled look at times gone by. Costumed actors play important personalities from Calgary's past, demonstrating and explaining the way things used to be in the "good ol' days." Visitors can stroll down Main Street and stop in at the shoe store, the old Calgary Herald office, North West Mounted Police jails, a general store that sells snacks and souvenirs, and much more. Hop aboard a 1920s-era streetcar and take a

☞ SEASONS AND TIMES

➛ General public: May—Oct, daily, 9 am—5 pm.
School groups: Fall, Winter and Spring. Call to reserve a tour.

☞ COST

➛ Adults $5.75, seniors $5, youths (7 to 17) $3.25, under 7 free.

☞ GETTING THERE

➛ Take 9th Ave. east just beyond 7th St. and turn left into the parking lot. About five minutes from the Calgary Tower.
➛ By public transit, take CT bus 1 (Forest Lawn) from 9th Ave. and Macleod Trail and ride it to Fort Calgary.
➛ By bicycle or on foot, take 9th Ave. east to 7th St. Fort Calgary is on your left.

☞ **NEARBY**

→ Billingsgate Fish Market, The Deane House, Inglewood Bird Sanctuary.

☞ **COMMENT**

→ Staff are trained in first aid procedures. Plan a half-day visit.

virtual tour of city streets or frolic in the vintage car. Kids love gathering 'round on an old-fashioned porch to listen to a docent tell tales from the old west. You can even learn how to build a log cabin.

When you're finished inside, head for the palisade (circa 1875) behind the museum. Volunteers using old-fashioned tools are reconstructing this log structure and they're more than happy to field questions from interested youngsters. Kids can avail themselves of the supplied mixture of mud and straw and hurl it at the wall, helping to cement the logs together. A windmill and a reconstructed version of the fort's 1888 barracks are also in the works.

Birthday parties and special events are staged on site in the summer. Fort Calgary also operates The Deane House, a restaurant in a charming historic house across the Elbow River on 9th Street. It's the closest place to go for lunch or tea before or after your visit.

History in the Making at HERITAGE PARK

1900 Heritage Dr.
Calgary
(403) 259-1900
www.heritagepark.ab.ca

This much-loved 27-hectare historic village provides visitors with a glimpse of life in Calgary pre-1914. Stroll the paths of the well-kept grounds and tour some of the city's oldest houses, fitted with antiques from the era. Visit businesses typical of Calgary circa 1910 on Main Street, pausing for a purchase at the old-fashioned Alberta Bakery. Get involved in lively interpretive talks and activities conducted by people in costume.

When little legs get tired, board the old-fashioned steam locomotive that crosses the park, or chug around Glenmore Reservoir on the *S.S. Moyie*, a sternwheeler boat (the higher park admission includes these rides; the lower one doesn't, but you can buy individual tickets for the rides inside the park). Or, hop onto a horse-drawn wagon and clip-clop through the streets. In the summertime, enjoy the antique midway with its gentle carousel, caterpillar ride

☞ Seasons and Times

→ Victoria Day weekend—July 1, Mon—Fri, 10 am—4 pm; weekends, 10 am—6 pm.
July 1 to Labour Day, daily, 10 am—6 pm.
Labour Day—Thanksgiving, weekends and holidays, 10 am—5 pm.
Mid-Nov—mid-Dec, weekends, 9 am—4 pm. Call for exact dates.

☞ Cost

→ Day pass (with and without midway, train and boat rides): Adults $18 and $11, children (3 to 17) $14 and $7, under 3 free.
Season's passes (with and without midway, train and boat rides): Adults $29 and $15, children (3 to 17) $23 and $10, families (two adults and dependent children) $99 and $47.

and boat-shaped swings for tots.

Home-style breakfast buffets are offered every Sunday in the Wainwright Hotel between mid-October and mid-May. The Fall Fair is held on Labour Day weekend and the Fall Harvest Festival the weekend after. Heritage Park is open during the Christmas season for holiday presentations and festivities.

☞ **Getting There**

→ By car, take 9th Ave. east to 1st St. S.E. and drive south, merging with Macleod Trail. Continue south on Macleod to Heritage Dr. then drive west until you reach 14th St. The park is straight ahead of you. Free parking on site. About 15 minutes from the Calgary Tower.

→ By public transit, take the LRT from 7th Ave. south to Heritage Station, then transfer to CT bus 502 (Heritage Park).

→ By bike, use the City of Calgary trails.

☞ **Comment**

→ A pancake breakfast, included with your admission, is served between 9 and 10 am in the Gunn's Dairy Barn. Plan a half-day visit.

Examining Calgary's Roots at TSUU T'INA MUSEUM

3700 Anderson Rd. S.W.
Calgary
(403) 238-2677

Tucked inside the cultural office in the Sarcee Seven Chiefs Sportsplex on the Tsuu T'ina Nation lands, is the Tsuu T'ina Museum. Native art, traditional costumes and stuffed versions of the animals hunted in the area by this Plains Indian band make up just some of the exhibits on display here.

Particularly interesting are artifacts such as the willow branch calendar used by one chief to mark the passage of time and traditional games that native children played a century ago. A teepee sits in the centre of the museum's back room.

For kids, taking a guided tour is more interesting because knowledgeable guides offer explanations about things such as Treaty 7, which the Tsuu T'ina believed was a peace treaty signed with the Government of Canada, while the government claimed the treaty turned over all Tsuu T'ina lands to Canada. Some items on display do not have explanatory panels nearby, so a guide would be most helpful.

The museum offers 45-minute tours for groups of 25 students. Tours of the 27,935 hectares of Tsuu T'ina lands beyond the confines of the museum, including historic sites and views of grazing buffalo, must be arranged through the Tourism Office (974-1400).

☞ SEASONS AND TIMES

➛ Year-round, Mon—Fri, 8:30 am—4:30 pm.

☞ COST

➛ $3 per person for a self-guided tour; $75 for a guided tour with 25 students or fewer.

☞ GETTING THERE

➛ By car, take 9th Ave. east to 1st St. S.E. and turn south, merging onto Macleod Trail. Follow Macleod south to Anderson Rd. and turn west, continuing along Anderson until it meets 37th St. The Tsuu T'ina lands are right in front of you. Pass the first building on your right and take the road to your right, following it to the Sarcee Seven Chiefs Sportsplex. Enter through the front doors and then turn right. The museum is located inside the Culture Office. Free parking on site. About 15 minutes from the Calgary Tower. There is no public transit to the reserve.

☞ COMMENT

➛ First aid is available through the arena office. Plan a 30-minute to 1-hour visit.

Giddyup to COCHRANE RANCHE PROVINCIAL HISTORIC SITE

Hwy. 1A at Hwy. 22
Cochrane
(403) 932-2902
www.gov.ab.ca/mcd/mhs/coch/coch.htm

Way back in 1881, Québec businessman M.H. Cochrane set up a ranch northwest of what would eventually be the city of Calgary, the first of the big leasehold ranches in the Canadian West. The Cochrane Ranch Company owned 76,518 wild hectares in the foothills. But two years later, brutal

Seasons and Times

➛ Visitor Centre: June 1—Labour Day, daily, 10 am—6 pm.
Ranche site: Year-round, daily.

Cost

➛ Visitor Centre: Adults $2, seniors and youths (7 to 17) $1.50, under 7 free, families (two adults and their children) $5.
Annual passes available.

Getting There

➛ By car, take Centre St. north to 6th Ave. and turn west. Follow 6th until it becomes Bow Trail. Follow Bow Trail west to Sarcee Trail and then turn north. Take the Hwy. 1 Exit west, then turn north onto Hwy. 22, following it until just beyond the spot where it meets up with Hwy. 1A. Free parking on site. About 40 minutes from the Calgary Tower.

Comment

➛ For up-to-date information, call (403) 932-3242 (operates in the summer only). The trails are not suitable for wheelchairs or strollers. A trip here is a perfect adjunct to a visit to the Western Heritage Centre (pages 47 and 181).

winters forced the company to leave the Big Hill site. The land remains one of the town of Cochrane's splendours, open to the public to wander and enjoy. From summer to early fall, the Visitor Centre is open, providing interpretive information. All year round, the trails invite the outdoor lover to explore and enjoy the area's beautiful vistas. Bring a picnic and then take a walk around the site, looking for the perfect spot to eat.

Other Historical Sites

Glenbow Museum

130 - 9TH AVE. S.E.
CALGARY
(403) 268-4100
WWW.GLENBOW.ORG

There's all kinds of history to be found at the Glenbow—art history, of course, in the galleries, as well as natural and geological history in the shapes of fossils and rocks in the permanent Treasures of the Mineral World exhibition. In the First Nations galleries, visitors can inspect traditional outfits, weapons, artifacts and artwork created by native peoples across Canada. Frequently, school groups are invited to sit inside the spectacular otter flag teepee of the Siksika Nation to hear stories that have been passed down for generations. Meanwhile, back at the ranching display, find out about rugged individuals such as John Ware, an ex-slave and highly respected cowboy, and Agnes Skrine, a freedom-loving Irish poet who ran a ranch in High River. Western paintings, bronze sculptures and photographs bring The Golden Age of Ranching exhibition to life.

In the Heritage From the Homeland gallery, learn fascinating history about the settlers who tamed the wild west. In the Growing Up and Away: Youth in Western Canada exhibition, today's kids will find old-fashioned toys, outfits and games (like a Hopscotch outline built into the carpet) that they can play. Youngsters can also climb on the go-cart at the entrance to the exhibition and use bins full of toys to create a toy display like those they see in the cases around them. There are also Q & A books about the exhibit that children can fill out to help them make the most of their visit. For more information on the Glenbow, turn to page 44 of this book.

☞ Year-round: Daily, 9 am—5 pm. (Thursdays and Fridays open until 9 pm.) Closed Christmas Day and New Year's.

☞ Adults $8, seniors and students $6, youths (6 to 12) $4, under 6 free, families $25 (maximum two adults and four children). Reduced admission Sunday before noon, and Thursday and Friday after 5 pm.

☞ From the Calgary Tower, cross 9th Ave. and walk east. You'll see the Glenbow on your left before you reach the corner.
By public transit, take CT bus 10, 9 or 4 and get off at the Municipal building on Macleod Trail and 8th Ave. Cross the street, walk west one block, and cross 1st St. S.E. The museum is on your left. By LRT, take the City Centre train and get off at 7th Ave. and 1st St. S.E. Walk south along 1st St. one block. The museum is on your right.

Western Heritage Centre

HWY. 22
ONE KILOMETRE NORTH OF COCHRANE
(403) 932-3514
WWW.WHCS.AB.CA

The history of ranching in the Calgary area is made vivid at the Western Heritage Centre in Cochrane. Children learn how ranching operations used to be carried out and discover through exciting hands-on exhibits what this rugged business encompasses today. They will even get to know what it's like to help a cow deliver her baby and how hard it is to rope a calf in a hurry.

Kids' programs at the Centre include A Night on the Range—a Western-style supper, a lesson in ranching activities, a bedtime snack and story, a campfire sing-along and a cowpoke breakfast. Call 932-3659 to book your group. For more information on the Western Heritage Centre, turn to page 47 in this book.

☞ Summer (Victoria Day to Thanksgiving): Daily: 9 am–5 pm.
Winter (Thanksgiving to Victoria Day): Thu–Sun, 9 am–5 pm.

☞ Adults $7.50, seniors (over 50) and students (12 to 17) $5.50, children (7 to 11) $3.50.
Annual passes and group discounts available.

☞ By car, take 9th Ave. east to 1st St. S.E. Turn south to 17th Ave. and drive west to Sarcee Trail. Turn north and follow it to the Hwy. 1 turnoff west to Banff and continue until you see the signs for Cochrane. Turn north onto Hwy. 22 and watch for the signs for the Western Heritage Centre turnoff, which is on your right. Free parking on site. About 30 minutes from the Calgary Tower.

Chapter 10

Getting There Is Half the Fun

Introduction

Sometimes the trip is as entertaining as the destination. That's especially true for children, who may never have passed between the portals of an airport, bought a ticket and boarded a C-Train or gone on a rustic horse-drawn wagon ride around a park. The Calgary area has its share of transportation options. Older kids will get the thrill of a lifetime from a balloon ride. Younger ones will relish a bike tour. A scamper through the Plus-15 system is the perfect way to get around the downtown core whatever the season. A sleigh ride in winter, a float around a peaceful lagoon in the early fall . . . pleasant diversions such as these definitely make getting there more than half the fun.

Note

You'll find these other fun ways to travel elsewhere in this guide:
White water rafting (Chapter 4, page 97)
Trail riding (Chapter 7, page 150 and Chapter 12, page 228)
Riding a steam locomotive and a sternwheeler (Chapter 9, page 175)
Dogsledding (Chapter 12, page 230)
Taking a train (Chapter 12, page 218)
Soaring in a gondola (Chapter 12, page 233)

Wheel through History MOUNTAIN CARRIAGE TOUR COMPANY

750 – 9TH AVE. S.E.
CALGARY
(403) 932-9876
WWW.CALGARYCARRIAGETOUR.COM

Rolling along in a horse-drawn wagon or carriage is a fun way to learn interesting tidbits about Calgary's early residents and colourful frontier past. The Mountain Carriage Tour Company offers sightseers a three-hour Historic Calgary Tour that starts in Inglewood, Calgary's first district, and moves on to Fort Calgary, site of the city's initial settlement. During the ride, experienced guides tell tales about passing points of interest and explain the history behind landmarks such as the old native encampment and the place where the North West Mounted Police first crossed the Bow River before setting up the fort in 1875. A short stop in Inglewood lets active kids stretch their legs while parents browse through some of the area's numerous antique shops. At Fort Calgary, disembark and explore the family-friendly interpretive centre. After the tour, you can check out the company's stables and meet some of the horses.

☞ SEASONS AND TIMES

➛ May—Oct, daily. Call for a complete tour schedule. Reservations are required for longer trips.

☞ COST

➛ Costs vary, but expect to pay at least $25 per carriage for a short evening tour and $48 per adult for a longer wagon tour (this price includes admission to Fort Calgary). Covered wagon and hay wagon tours of Fort Calgary are $5 per person.

☞ GETTING THERE

➛ Varies with the tour. Call for details.

Mountain Carriage Tours also offers shorter excursions around Fort Calgary on a covered wagon or hay wagon, and evening tours of Prince's Island Park in a carriage.

Elevated Entertainment CALGARY'S PLUS 15 SYSTEM

In Calgary, pedestrians can choose to stroll along at street level or breeze through covered bridges and walkways 15 feet (4.6 metres) above the ground. Dubbed the "+15 System," this popular network of indoor elevated sidewalks stretches for 16 kilometres and has 57 bridges linking office buildings and atriums in the downtown core.

SEASONS AND TIMES
➛ Year-round: Daily, generally during business hours only. Call 268-5354 for details.

COST
➛ Free.

COMMENT
➛ Maps located at regular intervals will help you to navigate the +15 System.

Bustling with energy in the daytime, the +15 System allows you and your kids to people-watch, among other pursuits. Take the time to linger at a few of the many atriums located along the circuit, some with gushing fountains, cascading waterfalls or quiet pools stocked with brightly coloured goldfish. Certain passages feature sculptures and murals, so you can even sneak a little culture into your kids' day. Younger children will enjoy spotting buses and trains from the bridges spanning 7th Avenue, or steer them to the Petro Canada Centre, where a bright yellow 1946 Norseman Mark V bush aircraft is poised to land in the lobby.

When you've had enough exploring for one day, head to one of the many eateries that dot the route. You're more likely to find seats if you arrive before noon.

Takeoff at CALGARY INTERNATIONAL AIRPORT

2000 Airport Rd. N.E.
(403) 735-1375
www.calgaryairport.com
www.space4kids.com

Canada's fourth busiest airport teems with interesting activities for kids, from watching the incoming baggage chug along on the carousel to gazing at giant airplanes as they take off. The airport offers tours for children that are full of fascinating facts, such as the nugget that Calgary has the longest civil aviation runway in Canada. KidsPort Day Tours always

Seasons and Times

Airport and KidsPort: Year-round, daily.
KidSpace: Call for hours.
Tours: Sept—mid-June, Mon—Fri.
KidsPort Day Tours take place at 9:30 am, School Day Tours at 9:20 am and Kids Evening Tours at 6:15 pm.

Cost

Airport, tours, KidsPort: Free.
KidSpace: Free. Simulator rides extra.

Getting There

➛ By car, take Centre St. north to 16th Ave. and turn east. Take Deerfoot Trail north to McKnight Blvd. and turn east. Take Barlow Trail north to Airport Rd., which curves west in front of the airport. Park in the public pay lot. About 25 minutes from the Calgary Tower.

➛ By public transit, take the Whitehorn train from anywhere on 7th Ave. to the Whitehorn Station, then transfer to CT bus 57, which will take you to the Arrivals level of the airport.

Nearby

➛ Aero Space Museum.

include a look at the main public areas in the terminal building followed by free time in the KidsPort play area, a mini airport equipped with an interactive control tower, airplane and play stations. "Snack for a Loonie" and free parking are also available if you're on a tour—call the Hospitality Relations office at 735-1375. KidsPort Evening Tours serve Guide and Scout groups. The airport also offers School Day Tours for students in grades 2 to 12. "Lunch for a Twoonie" and free parking can be arranged.

Even if you just want to explore the airport on your own, you're welcome to check out the KidsPort area (on the Departures level of the airport, near the Air Canada check-in). In September of 2000, a new hi-tech centre called KidSpace will open inside the main terminal on the mezzanine level. Focused on aviation, space exploration and the latest in communications technology, KidSpace will feature NASA exhibits and motion and flight simulator rides.

Take a Spin Around Calgary
CYCLE HIGH TOURS

G104 - 1919 UNIVERSITY DR. N.W.
CALGARY
(403) 283-9167 OR 1-800-461-5147

Kids love their bikes, so why not indulge them with a fun-filled spin around Calgary? Cycle High Tours offers many exciting family-oriented bike tours in and around the city. If you don't have the right equipment, Cycle High has helmets and mountain bikes to fit everyone, as well as bike trailers for toddlers. On longer trips they'll even pack you a lunch.

Families with younger children will enjoy the half-day Downtown/River Valley tour that winds through Calgary's many riverside parks. The area's ducks and geese are always a hit with little ones and, with frequent stops along the way, there's lots of opportunity for them to let off steam at the playgrounds. Older children with more stamina may enjoy riding to the Calgary Zoo (admission is included in the tour price), or the interpretive tour of Fish Creek Provincial Park where

☞ **SEASONS AND TIMES**

➛ April—Oct, daily. Call for details. Reservations are required.

☞ **COST**

➛ Costs vary, but expect to pay at least $15 per person for a half-day tour and $25 per person for a full-day tour. Drumheller and Kananaskis tours will cost more. Prices include transportation to and from the tour starting point (where applicable), mountain bike rentals, helmets, safety vests, an experienced guide and a lunch or snack when appropriate.

☞ **GETTING THERE**

➛ Varies with the tour. Call for details.

they'll spend a day exploring the park's unique flora and fauna with a knowledgeable guide. Adventurous riders will even get a chance to "off-road" on mountain bike trails.

Cycle High also offers a day trip through the mountains and a Drumheller Dinosaur Tour for kids smitten with dinosaurs (admission to the Royal Tyrrell Museum is included in the price). All tour guides are experienced and certified in first aid.

Take a Trip with CALGARY TRANSIT

240 – 7TH AVE. S.W.
CALGARY
(403) 262-1000
WWW.CALGARYTRANSIT.COM

SEASONS AND TIMES

➛ Year-round: Daily, generally 5 am—12:30 am.

COST

➛ Single Fare: Adults $1.60 (for the express bus add $0.50), youths (6 to 14) $1, under 6 free.
Book of 10 tickets: Adults $14.50, youths (6 to 14) $9.
Day passes: Adults $5, youths (6 to 14) $3.
Monthly passes: Adults $50, youths (6 to 14) $36, university students $45.
Annual passes for seniors: $35.

Whether you're heading downtown to a festival or across town to the zoo, Calgary Transit (CT) can turn an ordinary journey into an adventure. Younger kids will delight in everything from waiting at the bus stop or C-train station to ringing the bell at their destination. But the best part about using Calgary Transit is the interconnected bus and light rail (LRT) service, a fast and easy way to get to virtually any corner of the city. Keep your ticket or transfer to make the jump between modes of transport and remember that riding the LRT within the downtown core (between City Hall and 10th Street S.W.) is free.

> ☞ **Comment**
>
> ➛ Passengers must use exact change when paying cash fares or purchasing a ticket from a vending machine. ID cards are required when using passes and youth tickets.

If you miss your C-train, you won't have long to wait—trains run every five minutes during rush hour and every 15 minutes during non-peak hours. Taking the bus? Then call the Teleride number posted at your stop to find out when the next two or three buses will arrive. Whether you take the bus or the train, Calgary Transit's Park 'n' Ride lots make travelling convenient and accessible.

For transit maps and route schedules, call the Calgary Transit Customer Service Centre or visit its offices between 8:30 am and 5 pm at the address given above. Tickets and passes can be purchased at the service centre, as well as at C-train station concessions and some grocery, variety and drug stores.

Paddling Along at BOWNESS PARK

8900 – 48TH AVE. N.W.
CALGARY
(403) 221-3819

SEASONS AND TIMES
- Victoria Day weekend—Thanksgiving weekend, daily, 10 am—9 pm.

COST
- Prices for 30 minutes: Canoes $6, pedal boats (two and four-person) $6 and $10.

GETTING THERE
- By car, take Centre St. north to 16th Ave. and turn west. Continue along 16th Ave. past the Sarcee Trail Exit (it then becomes the Trans-Canada Hwy.) until you see Canada Olympic Park on your left. Turn north onto Bowfort Rd. and follow it until it becomes 83rd St. Turn west onto Bowness Rd. (which becomes 85th St.) and follow the signs to the park; it's on your left. Free parking on site. About 20 minutes from the Calgary Tower.
- By public transit, take CT bus 1 (Bowness) and ride it to the park.

NEARBY
- Riverside Playland.

COMMENT
- An adult must accompany small children on the boats. You'll need to leave something as a deposit, such as your driver's license. Take extra money with you for the Playland and ice cream.

Is there anything more calming than paddling a canoe? On a warm summer or fall day a paddle around the lagoon at Bowness Park is heavenly. The waterway is not large and it's impossible to get lost, so parent and child can practice those J-strokes and relish the joy of time spent on the water, surrounded by trees and the pleasurable sounds of summer. If it's a Saturday, you're likely to pass more than a few wedding parties posing for photos in this picturesque park. Feeling slightly more ambitious? Then rent a pedal boat (life jackets, which are required, are included in the rental cost) and get in a little leg exercise. This is bliss.

Go Walkabout on CALGARY'S PATHWAYS

Like to walk, run, cycle or in-line skate? Then Calgary's vast network of paved pathways is sure to delight—whether you're a toddler wobbling along on a tricycle or an athlete eating up the kilometres on a road bike. Over 223 kilometres of trails link the city's parks and natural areas, and many follow the scenic Bow and Elbow river valleys. Benches, picnic sites, playgrounds, drinking fountains, ice-cream trucks, concession stands and washrooms are located along many of the routes, though most concession stands and washrooms are only open in summer. In the wintertime, some of the more popular paths are maintained, such as those around Prince's Island Park.

> ☞ **SEASONS AND TIMES**
> ➛ Year-round. Some pathways are not cleared in the winter. Call 268-2300 to verify.
>
> ☞ **COST**
> ➛ Free.
>
> ☞ **COMMENT**
> ➛ Cyclists, in-line skaters and rollerskiers should wear an approved helmet that's properly fitted.

To help plan your trip, or trips, you can pick up a copy of the *Pathways and Bikeways* map ($1) at most Calgary bike shops. Wherever you go, watch for the entertaining and fun Travelling Pathway Show with its information on pathway safety, natural areas and outdoor recreational opportunities. Before you head out, make sure your bicycle is equipped with a horn or bell—it's a legal requirement.

Other Ways to Get There

Bus Tours

BREWSTER TOURS
808 CENTRE ST. S.E.
CALGARY
(403) 221-8242
WWW.BREWSTER.CA

Nothing beats a bus tour if you want an overview of Calgary area attractions. Brewster Tours offers a four-hour Calgary Sights Tour where you'll get a guided tour of the downtown area and its historic buildings, a tour inside and outside Fort Calgary, of Canada Olympic Park, the Jubilee Auditorium and the Olympic Oval at the University of Calgary. Brewster also offers guided trips that are farther afield. Prices vary.

☞ Calgary Sights Tour: Early May—early Oct, departs daily at 1:30 pm from the Brewster Office (808 Centre St. S.E.) at the Marriott Hotel.

☞ Calgary Sights Tour: Adults $47, children (5 to 11) $23.

Helicopter Rides

Some of Canada's most magnificent vistas are an hour's drive west of Calgary, and nature-lovers avail themselves of the chance to see the Rockies whenever possible. But hop aboard a helicopter and get an entirely different perspective of the city and its environs. This expensive but rare adventure is as exciting for children as it is for adults. While the average family isn't likely to make helicopter rides a regular occurrence, for a once-in-a-lifetime splurge, you can't beat this form of transportation. If you're already in the mountains on a visit, call local helicopter services there for information on tours. Trips are generally available year-round, depending on the weather.

Bighorn Helicopters
Calgary
(403) 286-7186

Typical route flies from Springbank Airport over Ghost Lake and the mountains of Kananaskis. Two adults and one child cost $575 per hour.

Canadian Helicopters Ltd.
Calgary
(403) 735-5914

Leaves from Calgary Airport for a 25-minute daytime air tour of the city. $500 for five people.

Turbowest Helicopters
Calgary
(403) 291-3855

Leaves from Calgary Airport for a 30-minute air tour of Calgary. $350 for four people.

Hot Air Balloons

Climb aboard a hot air balloon. When the sky is clear and the winds are calm, you can get a real bird's eye view of the city and the surrounding countryside. Professional pilots guide the flight, which generally lasts from 60 to 90 minutes. The entire experience, including balloon inflation, champagne picnic (juice and soda are available for the underage crowd) and return home takes about three hours. Listed below are some companies in the area that offer hot air balloon rides to high flyers aged ten and up. Trips are generally offered year-round, depending on the weather, and reservations are required.

Costs vary, but expect to pay at least $160 for a three-hour balloon ride. Prices usually include a champagne picnic and post-flight transportation.

Aerodynamics
102 - 4215 - 72nd Ave. S.E., Calgary
(403) 203-9310

Balloon Dimensions Inc.
1 - 5310 - 1st St. S.W., Calgary
(403) 254-5246

Balloons Over Calgary
7134 R. Fisher St. S.E., Calgary
(403) 259-3154

Sky's the Limit Balloons
4310 Macleod Trail S., Calgary
(403) 243-9215

CHAPTER 11

FAVOURITE FESTIVALS

Introduction

Festivals in Calgary tend to take place outdoors because everybody knows that on the finest days of the year, nobody is going to want to sit inside darkened theatres at the Arts Centre, the Jubilee or anywhere else. If the festival isn't entirely situated outside, it generally has a significant al fresco component. Even in January, Winterfest encourages families to get out and experience the cold (in a positive fashion, of course). In May, the International Children's Festival enchants kids with indoor performances and outdoor buskers, games and activities. When spring finally turns into summer, Prince's Island sets the stage for many of the city's most popular festivals—the Folk Festival, CariFest and Afrikadey! hog the sunniest weekends. Heading down to the island with a big blanket, a bunch of kids and a bag full of sun hats can prove to be a truly memorable experience. The Calgary Stampede is the city's biggest festival of all, often blessed with the best weather of the season. As summer turns to fall, the Hispanic Festival offers a spicy mix of song, dance and food in the Eau Claire area, while Barbecue on the Bow hosts a smoky BBQ competition that gets everyone, from tots to grandpas, salivating. By November, crowds are surging through Heritage Park, even on the coldest days, for The Twelve Days of Christmas. The happy spirit that permeates festivals inspires intrepid behaviour. Use this handy guide and mark your calendar.

Kid Around at CALGARY'S INTERNATIONAL CHILDREN'S FESTIVAL

Arts Centre and Olympic Plaza
Calgary
(403) 294-7414
www.calgarychildfest.org

At the Calgary International Children's Festival, children and adults of all ages can enjoy captivating performances from around the world. Music is always a big part of the festival; skilled entertainers coax melodies from all manner of instruments, from the very ancient to the just plain wacky. Some performances combine music with storytelling—it's the perfect way to hear legends of the past. A wide variety of theatrical productions will entertain older children. There's also juggling, comedy, dance, acrobatics, poetry and puppetry.

Can't decide which shows to take in? Be sure

Seasons and Times

➛ Late May, daily. Times vary, but generally Mon–Fri, 10 am–3 pm; weekends, 10 am–5 pm.

Cost

➛ Ticketed shows: $6.50 per person. Donate $30 or more to the festival and become a "Friend" of the festival, which entitles you to purchase tickets in advance for $4.99.
Outdoor activities: Free with purchase of a ticket to any mainstage show.

Getting There

➛ By car or on foot, take 9th Ave. east to Macleod Trail. The Arts Centre is on the northwest corner and Olympic Plaza is one block north on Macleod Trail. Pay parking is available at the Arts Centre (enter off Macleod Trail) or at City Hall (enter off 9th Ave. S.E.). Minutes from the Calgary Tower.

➛ By public transit, take the downtown LRT to the City Hall stop on the south side of 7th Ave. (or the Olympic Plaza stop on the north), and walk south to the Arts Centre on Macleod Trail. CT buses 10, 9, 4 and 31 all stop nearby.

> ☞ **NEARBY**
> ➛ Calgary Tower, W.R. Castell Public Library, Municipal Building, Glenbow Museum, Stephen Avenue Mall, Calgary Police Interpretive Centre.

you don't miss the Jigsaw Benefit Concert and Silent Auction, an extravaganza of music, dance, juggling and comedy. At the Silent Auction (all proceeds go to help economically disadvantaged children attend the festival) there's even an enticing table of tidbits at kid-friendly prices.

After the show, dash outside and join the fun at Olympic Plaza. All activities, from crafts and face painting to tales in the storytelling tent, are free to anyone who buys a ticket to a mainstage performance. Roving clowns, comedians and jugglers entertain festival-goers or kids can join in and play a variety of co-operative games and activities.

Flowery Frolics
FOURTH STREET LILAC FESTIVAL

4TH ST. BETWEEN 17TH AVE. AND ELBOW DR. S.W.
CALGARY
(403) 229-0902
4STREETCALGARY.COM

Given the vagaries of Calgary's weather, you never can tell whether the lilacs will be in bloom for the Fourth Street Lilac Festival. No matter. The event is still loads of fun, packed with between 25,000 and 50,000 Mission residents and people from elsewhere who just love the carnival atmosphere. The event kicks off at noon with a parade. There are 250 artisans selling their wares, along with food vendors, musicians playing on eight stages and buskers entertaining the masses. A children's area lets kids do the balloon bounce or test out the climbing wall. Lots of dogs attend this event with owners in tow; counting them up is a pleasant occupation for canine-loving youngsters.

Wear comfortable shoes and bring hats, sunscreen, sunglasses and sweaters. Bottled water is always a good idea on an excursion like this.

☞ **Seasons and Times**

➛ Late May, Sun, noon—5 pm.

☞ **Cost**

➛ Free. Food, purchases and use of the children's area cost extra.

☞ **Getting There**

➛ By car, take 9th Ave. east to 1st St. S.E. and drive south to 17th Ave. Turn west on 17th and proceed to 4th St. Parking is hard to find. About seven minutes from the Calgary Tower.

➛ By public transit, take CT bus 3 and get off on 17th Ave. near 4th St. S.W. By LRT, take the southbound train to the Victoria Park/Stampede Station and then transfer to CT 417 community shuttle (17th Ave.), and ride it to 4th St. (Check with Calgary Transit at 262-1000 before the festival to make sure the shuttle will be running.)

➛ By bicycle, take 9th Ave. west to 5th St. S.W. and turn south. Bike along 5th to 17th Ave. and turn east. Stop at 4th St.

Mellow Out at THE CALGARY FOLK FESTIVAL

PRINCE'S ISLAND PARK
CALGARY
(403) 233-0904
WWW.CALGARYFOLKFEST.COM

For over 20 years, the Calgary Folk Festival has provided a fabulous roundup of singers and musicians in a wide variety of styles at Prince's Island Park. These artists have included such stellar entertainers as Stan Rogers, Tom Paxton, Richard Thompson, Ani DiFranco, Ricki Lee Jones and Joan Baez. With 50 performers on six stages, workshops and jam sessions, there's a lot to hear at this four-day event.

When the weather is fine, Prince's Island is the nicest place in town to relax. Your family will enjoy hours of wonderful music that may be called "folk" but is actually an ever-changing blend of traditional roots, Celtic, world beat, blues, bluegrass, alternative, country and other forms. Children's interests are well served in the Family Area on Saturday and Sunday, where there's music, theatre, comedy and storytelling. Kids can also partake in juggling, painting, supervised games and other activities.

☞ SEASONS AND TIMES

➛ Early July, Thu, 4:30 pm—10 pm; Fri, 4:30 pm—11 pm; Sat, 10:30 am—11 pm; Sun, 10:30 am—10 pm.

☞ COST

➛ Adults $30 per evening or $35 full day, children under 14 free. No single day price for youths. Adult four-day pass $85 (if bought in advance, otherwise around $95 at festival time), youth four-day pass (14 to 17) $50. Tickets go on sale early in May.

They might also relish dancing to whatever's on the main stage, wandering through the clothing and jewellery in the Art Market kiosks and noshing on the various foods sold on-site. Older kids who've got their bearings can walk their siblings around to pick up a Popsicle or see what else is going on. There's a playground on the island outside the festival gates, but you can go in and out as you wish—if you have a stamp.

Bring a change of footwear, hats, sunscreen, mosquito repellent, warm clothes for the evening, waterproof ground cover and rain gear. No lawn chairs are allowed, so bring festival chairs only, with legs no longer than 20 centimetres.

GETTING THERE

➛ By car, take Centre St. north to 2nd Ave. Turn west and continue to 2nd St. S.W. where there's pay parking in the Eau Claire area. Walk over the bridge to the island. About ten minutes from the Calgary Tower.

➛ By public transit, take CT bus 31 (downtown shuttle; see note page 14) to Eau Claire Market and walk north to the park. By LRT, take the City Centre train and get off at 7th Ave. and 2nd St. S.W. Walk north along 2nd St. The market will be in front of you. Walk north along Barclay Parade and cross over the bridge to the park.

➛ By bike or on foot, take 9th Ave. west and turn north on 2nd St. S.W. Follow 2nd down Barclay Parade and veer left, going over the bridge to the island. Supervised bicycle parking is adjacent to the Festival entry gate (on the east side).

NEARBY

➛ Eau Claire YMCA, Chinatown, Eau Claire Market.

COMMENT

➛ A reserved, floored and covered area is available for physically challenged patrons and seniors. Gate drop-off can be arranged by calling 233-0904.

Git Along to
CANADA'S COWBOY FESTIVAL CHRISTMAS SHOW

TELUS CONVENTION CENTRE
120 - 9TH AVE. S.E.
CALGARY
1-800-822-2697
WWW.CALGARY-CONVENTION.COM

The Cowboy Festival has been around for six years; it now takes place for two days in early December. The purpose of the event is to preserve and perpetuate Calgary's Western heritage and to introduce young people to Western culture through dance, music, poetry, art and film. Historical displays

SEASONS AND TIMES

➛ Early Dec, Fri, noon—7:30 pm, evening concert, 8 pm—11 pm; Sat, 10 am—7:30 pm, evening concert, 8 pm—11 pm; Sun, 10 am—5 pm

COST

➛ Varies. Call the festival or visit its Web site, listed above.

GETTING THERE

➛ By car, take 9th Ave. east to Centre St., turn south into the Calgary Tower parking lot and park. The Convention Centre is one block east.

➛ By public transit, CT buses 10 or 31 will let you out on 9th Ave., close to the Convention Centre's south entrance. By LRT, take any downtown train and get off at 7th Ave. and 1st St. S.E. Walk south one block and east for a half a block on 8th Ave. to enter the building through its north entrance.

➛ By bicycle, use the car directions and park your bike on Stephen (8th) Ave.

NEARBY

➛ Calgary Tower, Olympic Plaza, Stephen Avenue Mall, W.R. Castell Public Library, Municipal Building, Glenbow Museum, Calgary Police Interpretive Centre.

are part of the set-up; so are booths featuring cowboy crafts, Western art, saddles, spurs, Western clothing, Aboriginal items and foods. There's even information about the history of the RCMP and the NWMP.

Feel the Warmth at WINTERFEST

VARIOUS VENUES AROUND CALGARY
(403) 543-5480
WWW.DISCOVERCALGARY.COM/WINTERFEST

It's Winterfest! Join in the fun as Calgary comes alive to celebrate all the season has to offer. There are winter sport competitions for all levels, ice sculptures and even curling championships. Unlike regular curling, however, this human version sees competitors lie on large inner tubes and send themselves spinning toward the target at the far end of the rink.

Families with kids should make straight for the Winterfest Fun Zone at Eau Claire Market. Here, children can play an impromptu game of street

☞ SEASONS AND TIMES

➛ Early Feb—mid-Feb, daily. Times vary, but generally, 11 am—4 pm.

☞ COST

➛ Free for most activities.

☞ GETTING THERE

➛ By car or on foot, take 9th Ave. east to Macleod Trail and go north. Head west on Riverfront Ave. to Eau Claire Market. Pay parking is available. Minutes from the Calgary Tower.

➛ By public transit, take CT bus 31 (downtown shuttle; see note page 14) to Eau Claire Market. By LRT, take the City Centre train and get off at 7th Ave. and 2nd St. S.W. Walk north along 2nd St. The market will be in front of you.

➛ On foot, take 9th Ave. west and turn north on 2nd St. S.W. Follow 2nd down Barclay Parade.

hockey, have their faces painted, make their way through a maze or try their hand at a variety of crafts. In past years, hay rides and a stage full of children's entertainers have also proved popular. Keep an eye out for performing clowns and make sure to say hello to Chinook, Winterfest's snowy owl mascot.

Leave time for Prince's Island Park; for part of this festival the park is transformed into a winter wonderland. Kids can try out snowshoes or cross-country skis, sample maple candy made in the traditional way (by pouring hot syrup over snow), watch an igloo being built or scurry through an obstacle course. Some years the park sports a teepee village, where festival-goers can watch traditional native dancing and learn more about the Blackfoot culture. Of course, no winter day would be complete without steaming mugs of hot chocolate, sipped close to a crackling fire.

Other Favourite Festivals

The Calgary Stampede

1410 Olympic Way S.E.
(403) 261-0101
Calgary
www.calgary-stampede.com

Calgary's major festival is the annual Stampede. At Stampede Park, you'll find the rodeo and chuckwagon races, the midway, Indian Village, agricultural exhibitions, pig races, Stampede Grandstand Show and fast food galore, but all that'll cost you. There are many free events outside the grounds. For instance, there are several free pancake breakfasts put on around the city every day. At these events, sometimes there are free pony rides for kids, too. Check your favourite newspaper for details.

When you just can't eat another pancake, mosey along downtown's Stephen Avenue Mall in search of square dancing demonstrations and live music. At nighttime, look for a free spot on Scotsman's Hill or another good vantage point and enjoy the fireworks that follow every evening's Stampede Grandstand Show. Don't miss the Stampede Parade too, on the first Friday of the festival. You can yee-haw 'till the cows come home. See page 34 for more details on the Stampede and events.

☞ Early July—mid-July.
Stampede Grounds: 11 am—midnight. Grounds open at 9 am on Family Day, Kids Day and other special days. Check the newspapers or Stampede booklet for details.

☞ For many events outside the grounds: Free.
General admission to Stampede Park: Adults (13 to 64) $9, seniors (65 and up) and children (7 to 12) $4, under 7 free. There are deals available and some activities have additional costs.

☞ By car, take 9th Ave. east to 1st St. S.E. and go south until 1st meets Macleod Trail. The Stampede Grounds are on your left. Look for parking on neighbouring streets; expect to pay jacked-up rates. About seven minutes from the Calgary Tower.
By public transit, take any LRT to Victoria Park Stampede Station. Or take CT bus 10 (Southcentre), which drops you off at the corner of 1st St. and 17th Ave. S.E. Take the pedestrian walkway over to the park.
By bicycle or on foot, use the car directions. There are bicycle racks at the entrances.

Carifest Caribbean Festival

VARIOUS DOWNTOWN LOCATIONS, INCLUDING PRINCE'S ISLAND
(403) 292-0310

Rich, happy sounds fill the city centre during Carifest, a festival of music and dance from the Caribbean, which kicks off with a downtown parade. The most inviting part of the festival for many families is the day at Prince's Island, where vendors sell wonderful Caribbean food and a series of bands takes the main stage. Call for details and cost of admission.

☞ Mid-June.

☞ To get to Prince's Island by car, take Centre St. north to 2nd Ave. Turn west and continue to 2nd St. S.W. where there's pay parking in the Eau Claire area. Walk over the bridge to the island. About ten minutes from the Calgary Tower.
By public transit, take CT bus 31 (downtown shuttle; see note page 14.) to Eau Claire Market and walk north to the park. By LRT, take the City Centre train and get off at 7th Ave. and 2nd St. S.W. Walk north along 2nd St. The market will be in front of you. Walk north along Barclay Parade and cross over the bridge to the park.

Calgary International Jazz Festival

VARIOUS VENUES AROUND CALGARY
(403) 249-1119

Free, outdoor jazz concerts as well as indoor ticketed venues. The festival does not offer anything specifically for kids, but the whole family can enjoy the festival's free downtown concerts held daily on two moveable stages between 11:30 am and 1:30 pm on Stephen Avenue Mall.

☞ Late June—early July.

☞ Cost varies, depending on the venue and the performer. Outdoor concerts on Stephen Avenue Mall are free.

☞ By car or on foot, take 9th Ave. east to Macleod Trail. Pay to park underneath the Arts Centre on the northwest corner and walk up Macleod to 8th Ave. Follow 8th Ave. west to the closest outdoor stage.
By public transit, take the downtown LRT to the City Hall stop on the south side of 7th Ave., and walk south to Stephen Ave. CT buses 10, 9, 4 and 31 all stop nearby.

Kite Day

SOUTH GLENMORE PARK
90TH AVE. AND 35TH ST. S.W.
CALGARY
(403) 221-3530

On Father's Day every year, City of Calgary Parks and Recreation hosts Kite Day. With the materials provided on-site, children will be able to make and decorate kites and other wind-related crafts. Activities vary each year, but can include performers and displays. Many families bring their own kites with them. There's usually a concession for buying snacks, and there are always bathrooms available. Paths in the park allow families to set off on a walk, as well. Packing a picnic would allow you to make an entire afternoon of this event.

☞ Father's Day, 1–4 pm.

☞ Free.

☞ By car, take Centre St. north to 6th Ave. and turn west. Follow 6th until it turns into Bow Trail. Take the Crowchild south Exit and follow it to the Glenmore Trail west Exit. Take Glenmore Trail to the 14th St. S. Exit and drive south, past Glenmore Landing Shopping Mall to 90th Ave. Turn west on 90th and drive to 35th St. Turn right into the park. Free parking.
By public transit, take the downtown C-Train south to Heritage Station and then transfer to the CT 80 bus, which stops right near the park.

Afrikadey!

VARIOUS LOCATIONS AROUND CALGARY
(403) 234-9110
WWW.AFRIKADEY.ORG

Week-long festival of music, dance, visual arts, theatre and poetry from Africa and the Diaspora. Kids' programs in drumming. Most events take place downtown; last day takes place at Prince's Island Park, from 10 am to 8 pm. Check the Web site for details. Some events are free, some charge admission.

☞ Mid-August.

☞ Cost varies. Call for details.
Prince's Island: Adults $10, teens (12 to 18) $5, seniors and children under 12 free.

☞ To get to Prince's Island by car, take Centre St. north to 2nd Ave. Turn west and continue to 2nd St. S.W. where there's pay parking in the Eau Claire area. Walk over the bridge to the island. About ten minutes from the Calgary Tower.
By public transit, take CT bus 31 (downtown shuttle; see note page 14) to Eau Claire Market and walk north to the park. By LRT, take the City Centre train and get off at 7th Ave. and 2nd St. S.W. Walk north along 2nd St. The market will be in front of you. Walk north along Barclay Parade and cross over the bridge to the park.

Tsuu T'ina Nation Rodeo

TSUU T'INA RESERVE
REDWOOD MEADOWS, HWY. 22
CALGARY
(403) 281-4455

Rodeo and Indian Days Powwow, golf tournament, baseball tournament and sometimes there are rides for children. Kids can participate in sheep-riding (bring your own helmets). There are lots of aboriginal foods for sale.

☞ Last weekend in July.

☞ Powwow: Free.
Rodeo: Adults $7, seniors and kids under 6, free.

☞ Take Centre St. north to 16th Ave. and turn west. Follow 16th (which becomes Hwy. 1) west and turn north onto Hwy. 22, following it until you see the Redwood Meadows Golf and Country Club. The rodeo is held across Hwy. 22 from the golf club. Free parking on site.

Hispanic Festival

237 - 8TH AVE. S.E.
VARIOUS LOCATIONS AROUND CALGARY, INCLUDING THE EAU CLAIRE MARKET
(403) 271-2744
WWW.HISPANICARTS.COM

Concerts, dance performances and visual art—on a Hispanic theme, in the Hispanic tradition, or by Hispanic artists—are presented around town. On the weekend, the Eau Claire area becomes a hotbed of Hispanic food, arts and crafts, and performances of music and dance. Listen to mariachi singing and Romantic trios; watch flamenco, folk and salsa dancers. Experience the sizzling hot culture of Cuba, Brazil, Mexico, Chile and other Latin countries.

☞ Events at the Eau Claire Market are free. There is a cost for food and purchases. Other events may have a cost associated with them; call the number above for details.

☞ To get to Eau Claire by car, take Centre St. north to 2nd Ave. Turn west and continue to 2nd St. S.W. where there's pay parking in the Eau Claire area. About ten minutes from the Calgary Tower.
By public transit, take CT bus 31 (downtown shuttle; see note page 14) to Eau Claire Market. By LRT, take the City Centre train and get off at 7th Ave. and 2nd St. S.W. Walk north along 2nd St. The market will be in front of you.
By bike or on foot, take 9th Ave. west and turn north on 2nd St. S.W. Follow 2nd down Barclay Parade.

Festival on the Bow

PRINCE'S ISLAND PARK
CALGARY • (403) 225-1913

Barbecue competition begins Saturday night and is judged Sunday afternoon; there are children's activities on-site as well. In the past, the Calgary Philharmonic Orchestra has performed classical music live. Admission to the park is free during the day; there's a cost for the evening concerts.

☞ Labour Day weekend. Call for times.

☞ Admission to the park is free during the day.

TransAlta's Wildlights

CALGARY ZOO AND BOTANICAL GARDENS
CALGARY • (403) 232-9300

Spectacular lighting display and children's activities at the Calgary Zoo in the evenings through the Christmas season and into January. Should not be missed by families.

☞ Late Nov—early Jan.

☞ Adults $7, children $5.

Twelve Days Of Christmas

HERITAGE PARK
CALGARY • (403) 259-1900

On the weekends the park is open for families to build crafts, shop for crafts, carol in St. Martin's church, listen to stories at Weedon School and enjoy horse-drawn sleigh rides. The Wainwright Hotel is open for breakfast or lunch.

☞ Mid-Nov—late Dec: weekends, 9 am—4 pm.

☞ $2 per person or $5 per family. Free entry coupons are available at Safeway stores and First Calgary Savings Banks.

CHAPTER 12

FARTHER AFIELD

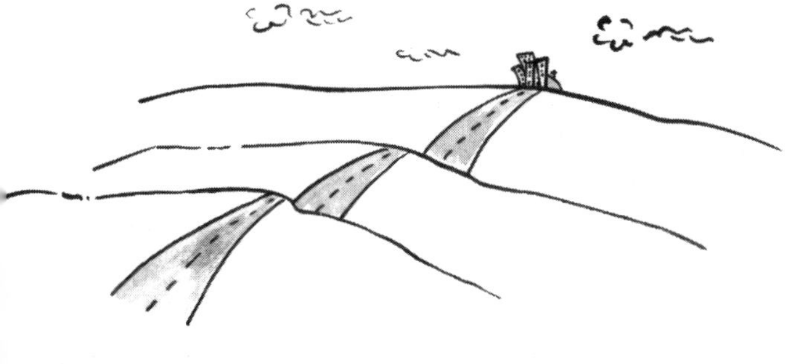

Introduction

When the weekend looms, many Calgarians like to head for the hills and enjoy the great outdoors. The Rockies are our playground, and with vistas such as those from the Banff Springs Hotel and Chateau Lake Louise to consider, who wants to stay home and watch cartoons? Skiing and snowboarding beckon the adventurous in the wintertime. Others enjoy a walk through an icy canyon or a trip by dogsled along a frosty trail. When summer finally arrives, there are fields full of wildflowers to investigate, canoes to paddle around tranquil mountain lakes and horses to ride along slender riverside trails. Some of Southern Alberta's most interesting museums are scattered outside the city's confines as well. Drive through the eerie badlands to the Royal Tyrrell Museum of Paleontology, a must-see for any family with an interest in dinosaurs. The Buffalo Nations Luxton Museum in Banff pays tribute to the heritage of the First Nations of the Northern Plains and Canadian Rockies. Hike the trails of Kananaskis, watch a live wild horse show and buffalo chase near Fort Macleod, ride an old-time steam train out of Stettler with teddy bears in tow or whip down winding waterslides at Sylvan Lake. There's no excuse for being bored when you live in Southern Alberta.

Natural History 101
BANFF PARK MUSEUM NATIONAL HISTORIC SITE

BANFF AVE. AND BUFFALO ST.
BANFF
(403) 762-1566
WWW.WORLDWEB.COM/PARKSCANADA-BANFF

Almost 100 years old, the Banff Park Museum is as compelling for its rustic wooden building as it is for its animal exhibits. One of Western Canada's first natural history museums, its unusual architecture recalls the train stations of yore; its glass-sided roof pagoda brought light into the museum before electricity came to Banff. Inside, encased in wavy old glass, there are stuffed specimens of a vast array of local animals and birds and dried examples of the numerous insects, including butterflies. Swans, eagles, mountain goats and bighorn sheep, grizzly and cinnamon bears, grey wolves, silver-haired bats and a surprisingly large beaver, all are presented in life-like fashion here. Some were once residents of the Banff Park Zoo, which operated from 1904 to 1937. The

SEASONS AND TIMES
→ Year-round: Daily, 1 pm—5 pm.

COST
→ Adults $2.50, students $2, youths $1.50, families $5.75.

GETTING THERE
→ Take Centre St. north to 16th Ave. and turn west. Follow 16th (which turns into Hwy. 1) to the Banff/Lake Minnewanka turnoff and turn south, into the town of Banff. Follow Banff Ave. to Buffalo St. Turn right and park in the Banff Park free lot. Walk across the park to the museum, which is just off Banff Ave. About 90 minutes from the Calgary Tower.

museum's Discovery Room allows children some hands-on activity, including handling artifacts such as sheep horns. There are also games, puzzles, books, animal pelts and videos to enhance the children's visit.

NEARBY

→ Luxton Museum, Whyte Museum of the Canadian Rockies.

COMMENT

→ You'll find restaurants and picnic areas nearby. Plan a 1-hour visit.

Enjoy Majestic Beauty THE BANFF SPRINGS HOTEL

405 SPRAY AVE.
BANFF
(403) 762-2211
WWW.FAIRMONT.COM

The closest building you'll find to a castle in Western Canada, the Banff Springs Hotel is a magnificent edifice with all kinds of crannies of interest to children. Its remarkable view of the Bow Valley is free; so is the use of its skating rink and tobogganing hills in winter. Amble through the hotel's public areas and examine its architecture and antique furnishings. Let the children scamper through the halls and down the mysterious staircases. Have a snack or a meal in one of the hotel's 17 restaurants and lounges (the Springs' groaning Sunday brunch buffet is legendary). Splurge and use the hotel's 32-metre swimming pool, which has handsome indoor and heated outdoor components, or take advantage of its Bowling Centre or Siding 29 Games Café in the Conference Centre across the street from the hotel. The Banff Springs is considered one of the most visually stunning hotels in the world. Even if you and your family aren't staying there, it's a national treasure that can't fail to charm even the most jaded child.

☞ Seasons and Times

➤ Hotel: Year-round, daily.
Swimming pool (unsupervised): Daily, 6 am–10 pm.
Bowling Centre: Daily. Call 762-6892.
Siding 29 Games Café: Daily, 10 am–2 am.

☞ Cost

➤ Swimming pool: $10 per person.
Bowling: Adults $3.75, seniors (55 and up) and children (under 11) $3.60, under 3 free. (Neon bowling: $24.50 per hour, maximum six people per lane.) Shoe rentals $1.10 per person.
Games Café: Admission is free; games extra.

☞ Getting There

➤ Take Centre St. north to 16th Ave. and turn west, following 16th (which becomes Hwy. 1) west to Banff. Take the Lake Minnewanka/Banff turnoff south into Banff and follow Banff Ave. over the bridge. Then veer left onto Spray Ave. and follow it to the end. Public pay parking is on your right, beyond the Recreation Complex. About 90 minutes from the Calgary Tower.

☞ Nearby

➤ Elbow Falls, Phil's Pancake House.

Similar Attraction

CHATEAU LAKE LOUISE
111 Lake Louise Dr.
Lake Louise
(403) 522-3511
WWW.FAIRMONT.COM

One of the most arresting vistas in the world, Lake Louise has plenty to engage the little ones, from canoeing in summer on the extraordinary turquoise glacial lake to walking along lakeside trails at any time of the year. In the winter, sleigh rides, snowshoeing expeditions and cross-country skiing beckon. In mid-January, the Chateau's grounds are transformed into an icy fantasy during the Ice Magic International Ice Sculpting Competition, which kicks off the annual Banff/Lake Louise Winter Festival. Chateau Lake Louise, a grand hotel, offers interpretive guides and mountaineers for local hikes. The hotel's many restaurants and lounges make an ideal spot to rest after all that fresh air. Weather is highly changeable in the mountains, no matter what the season; be sure to have warm clothes on hand for everyone. Take a camera and lots of film. The hotel is wheelchair and stroller accessible but the hiking trails are not.

All Aboard! ALBERTA PRAIRIE STEAM TOURS

STETTLER
(403) 742-2811
WWW.NUCLEUS.COM/HEARTLAND

For kids who love trains, a day spent chugging through the prairies of central Alberta is a day like no other. Alberta Prairie Steam Tours runs more than 60 excursions each summer that vary in length from five to eight hours.

Small children will be delighted by the Teddy Bear Specials: clowns and other kids' entertainers join your family on board and the trip includes a parade for tots and their very special friends. Older children may prefer the Red Coat Special, featuring members of the RCMP, or the Heritage Days Special, which includes admission to Stettler's annual fair. The Family Picnic excursion is a day out for every member of the family. On some trips, a train robbery or Wild West gunfight is a big part of the fun.

When kids need a change of pace from the live commentary and other on-board action, take them to the padded children's play area. The observation car is another popular spot: when the track curves you may catch a glimpse of the 1920s steam locomotive that powers the train (a 1958 diesel is occasionally used as well). Built from 1919 to the 1950s, the coaches are also vintage and beautifully restored. Two concession areas and a full beverage service help keep hunger at bay.

☞ SEASONS AND TIMES

➛ May—Oct, weekends and some weekdays. Call for a complete excursion schedule. Reservations are required.

☞ COST

➛ Costs vary, but expect to pay at least $60 per adult and $29.50 per child (4 to 10). Children under 3 free, but they may not be assigned a seat. On most excursions, a roast beef dinner is included in the fare.
Family Special: $150 for a family of four.
Teddy Bear Specials: Children (under 11) free if they bring a teddy bear.

☞ GETTING THERE

➛ Excursions depart from, and return to, the Stettler Station. By car, take 9th Ave. east to Macleod Trail and go north. Turn east on 5th Ave., stay to the right and head east on Memorial Dr. At Deerfoot Trail (its name changes to Hwy. 2) head north to Lacombe and go east on Hwy. 12. Continue into Stettler on Hwy. 12. The station is at the base of Stettler's yellow grain elevator. Free parking on site. About two and a half hours from the Calgary Tower.

A Traditional Roundup LIVE WILD HORSE SHOW AND BUFFALO CHASE

HWY. 3 (WEST OF FORT MACLEOD)
(403) 381-3889

Before the arrival of the horse, the Blackfoot people used buffalo jumps to hunt buffalo and dogs to help them transport their belongings from place to place. Eventually, they tamed the horse and learned to work with it to hunt buffalo. Operated by Sundance Traditional Tours, the live wild horse show and buffalo chase tells this story. Nightly performances include a history of the Blackfoot people and the horse, a wild horse roundup, a saddle bronc competition, a bare-back riding competition, a warrior skills display and a re-enactment of a traditional buffalo chase.

Adventurous families may also want to sign up for the overnight camping package. It includes the show, a basic riding lesson, trail rides led by experienced guides, a dinner of authentic cuisine, storytelling by elders around the campfire and traditional teepee accommodation. Sundance offers guided trail rides, too, that last from one hour to a full day. As you ride, enjoy learning about the history of the Old Man

SEASONS AND TIMES

➛ First Friday in June until Labour Day weekend. Daily, 6 pm–7 pm. Weather dependent.

COST

➛ Wild horse show: Adults (16 to 54) $13, seniors $10, children (5 to 15) $6, under 5 free, families $30.
Trail rides: From $20 per person (one-hour ride) to $85 per person (full-day ride).
Camping: $100 per person, $185 per couple.

River basin and its landmarks. Reservations are required for camping and trail rides.

GETTING THERE

→ By car, take 9th Ave. east to 1st St. S.E. (its name changes to Macleod Trail, then to Hwy. 2) and go south. At Hwy. 3 head west for approximately 13 kilometres. Free parking on site. About two hours from the Calgary Tower.

NEARBY

→ Head-Smashed-In Buffalo Jump Interpretive Centre, The Fort: Museum of the North West Mounted Police.

Dig Dinosaurs at THE ROYAL TYRRELL MUSEUM OF PALEONTOLOGY

HWY. 838
MIDLAND PROVINCIAL PARK
DRUMHELLER
1-888-440-4240 OR (IN ALBERTA, TOLL-FREE) 310-0000, ASK FOR 823-7707
WWW.TYRRELLMUSEUM.COM

Located on a World Heritage site in the visually striking badlands of Drumheller, the Royal Tyrrell Museum of Paleontology is a public and academic institution that attracts hundreds of thousands of visitors annually from around the globe. You

SEASONS AND TIMES

→ Victoria Day weekend—Labour Day, Mon—Sun, 9 am—9 pm. Labour Day—Thanksgiving, Mon—Sun, 10 am—5 pm. Thanksgiving—Victoria Day weekend, Tue—Sun, 10 am—5 pm. Open holiday Mondays.

☞ COST
➛ Adults $6.50, seniors (65 and up) $5.50, youths (7 to 17) $3, under 7 free, families (maximum two adults with accompanying children) $15. Tuesday admissions are half price in the winter. Two-day passes and group discounts are available.

☞ GETTING THERE
➛ Take Centre St. north to 16th Ave. and turn east. Follow 16th Ave. (which turns into Hwy. 1) east and then turn north at Hwy. 56. The Royal Tyrrell Museum is located in Midland Provincial Park. Follow the signs from Drumheller. The six kilometre drive from Drumheller to the museum follows the North Dinosaur Trail (Hwy. 838), a popular sightseeing route. About an hour and a half from the Calgary Tower.

☞ NEARBY
➛ Dinosaur Provincial Park, Midland Provincial Park, Horseshoe Canyon, Horsethief Canyon, Hoodoos Recreation Area

☞ COMMENT
➛ Call ahead to reserve an audio tape guide. Take sturdy walking shoes, sun hats, sunscreen and water so walks in the area will be possible. Wheelchairs and strollers (free) at the information desk. Plan a 2 to 6-hour visit, depending on your children's level of interest and ages.

can't beat it for scientific insights, as a cruise through its informative Web site beforehand quickly reveals. The museum is named for geologist Joseph Burr Tyrrell, who discovered the first dinosaur remains in the area and sparked the Great Canadian Dinosaur Rush.

At the Tyrrell, the beginnings of life are revealed through the displays of fossilized remains and traces of ancient plants and animals. Hands-on exhibits introduce visitors to basic concepts such as buoyancy, viscosity and mimicry by animals in the wild, important information that will help you to understand later exhibits. While the Dinosaur Hall, with its spectacular dinosaur skeletons (almost 40 in total, including one of a *Tyrannosaurus Rex*), is likely to be the climax of a visit to the museum, there are many other highlights. These include peering through the window to the preparation lab, where "preparators" carefully extract fossils from hunks of rock; walking through the Devonian Lakes section with its glass floor looking down into a recreation of ancient marine life; and inspecting the museum's great variety of fossils.

There are lots of educational programs at this museum, from organized Day Digs to scrounge for fossils (book early) to Dig Watch tours, to Summer Vacation Day Camps for kids 7 to 12. Make sure to budget some time to drive the area's well-marked Dinosaur Trail, getting out at the viewpoints and enjoying the strange, brief phenomenon of the free ferry across the Red Deer River.

Dinosaur Provincial Park, located a half-hour northeast of Brooks, encompasses over 7,000 hectares of badlands and prairie and is a UNESCO World Heritage Site. For information on guided tours and fossil safaris there (unguided hikes are not permitted in the natural preserve), call (403) 378-4342. Or, visit www.gov.ab.ca/env/parks/prov parks/ dinosaur

Back in the Saddle Again
BAR U RANCH NATIONAL HISTORIC SITE

Longview
1-800-568-4996
http://parkscanada.pch.gc.ca/parks/alberta/bar_u_ranch

Between 1882 to 1950, the Bar U Ranch was one of Canada's major ranching operations, internationally known as a centre of breeding excellence for cattle and purebred Percheron horses.

☞ **Seasons and Times**
➛ Victoria Day to Thanksgiving, daily, 10 am–6 pm.

☞ **Cost**
➛ Visitor Orientation Centre and site: Adults $6, seniors (65 and up) $5, youths (6 to 16) $3, under 6 free, families $14.50. Reduced rates for Orientation Centre only. Customized tours are available at various costs.

☞ **Getting There**
➛ Take 9th Ave. east to 1st St. S.E. and turn south. Follow 1st as it merges into Macleod Trail, which then becomes Hwy. 2. Take Hwy. 2 south to Hwy. 540, just after High River, and go west on the 540 to the Bar U. You will cross over Hwy. 22. Free parking on site. About 90 minutes from the Calgary Tower.

☞ **Nearby**
➛ Chain Lakes Provincial Park, Head-Smashed-In Buffalo Jump, High River, Kananaskis Provincial Park, Longview, Nanton, Okotoks.

☞ **Comment**
➛ The Friends of the Bar U offers tours to a number of ranches by bus ($85 per person minimum). To book, call 403-395-3993 or 403-652-5643. Plan a 1 to 2-hour visit.

Situated in the foothills, on the banks of Pekisko Creek, the Bar U included ranches on shortgrass prairie as well as farms, meat-packing factories and flour mills.

Nowadays, the place is operated by Parks Canada as a National Historic Site and offers visitors interpretive displays and guided tours. Families are invited to visit the Orientation Centre's Range Land exhibit and watch an award-winning video about the Bar U. Wander around Pekisko Creek General Store and grab a country-style lunch at the Bar U Roadhouse. Then, explore the spread on foot or by horse-drawn wagon ($3 per person), and learn about the people who lived and worked there. You may encounter one of the roving interpreters or happen upon a demonstration of traditional ranching techniques.

Seasonal activities include demonstrations of cow branding, roping and old-fashioned haying practices, and there are rodeo events, cowboy poetry and a roundup camp. Educational programs and Group Tour Adventures are offered. Special events like the Old Tyme Ranch Rodeo happen on weekends and holidays—check the Web site or call for details. Take your camera, wear sensible shoes and pack extra clothing; the weather can turn quickly.

Hard Living and Heroism at the Fort
MUSEUM OF THE NORTH WEST MOUNTED POLICE

219 - 25TH ST.
FORT MACLEOD
(403) 553-4703
WWW.DISCOVERALBERTA.COM/FORTMUSEUM

Directed to thwart whiskey traders and bring order to the lawless Canadian West in the late 1800s, the North West Mounted Police (now the RCMP) trekked 2,000 kilometres under the direction of Assistant Commissioner James Macleod. At the end of that journey, they built Fort Macleod.

The Fort Museum is a replica of that first outpost: through pictures, artifacts and excerpts of letters kids will learn about the lives led by both officers and enlisted men. There's

SEASONS AND TIMES

→ Spring (early May—late June) and Fall (early Sept—mid-Oct): Daily, 9 am—5 pm.
Summer (early July—late Aug): Daily, 9 am—8:30 pm.
Winter (mid-Oct—late Apr): Mon—Fri, 10 am—4 pm. Closed late Dec—late Feb.

COST

→ Adults $4.50, seniors $4, youths (12 to 17) $2.50, children (6 to 11) $1.50, under 6 free, families $14.

information on the history of the force as well as exhibits such as First Nations decorative work. Other buildings in the fort include a chapel similar to those that dot southern Alberta, a dispensary with displays of early medical instruments and Kanouse House, once the site of a trading post.

While school-aged children will get the most out of the exhibits, everyone is sure to enjoy the scaled-down version of the RCMP musical ride that's performed four times daily in July and August. Afterward, head to the stables for a closer look at the horses and a chat with the riders. Before you hop back into your car, go for a stroll down Fort Macleod's main street: over 30 restored buildings, including the old town jail and the haunted Empress theatre, date from between 1890 and 1920.

☞ Getting There

→ By car, take 9th Ave. east to 1st St. S.E. (its name changes to Macleod Trail, then to Hwy. 2) and go south. At Hwy. 3 head east to Fort Macleod. Turn north on 3rd Ave. and continue two blocks to Hwy. 3, heading west. Free parking on the left. About two hours from the Calgary Tower.

☞ Nearby

→ Head-Smashed-In Buffalo Jump Interpretive Centre, Live Wild Horse Show and Buffalo Chase.

☞ Comment

→ Plan a 2-hour visit.

Thunder over to HEAD-SMASHED-IN BUFFALO JUMP INTERPRETIVE CENTRE

FORT MACLEOD
(403) 553-2731
WWW.HEAD-SMASHED-IN.COM

A UNESCO World Heritage Site, Head-Smashed-In Buffalo Jump is one of the largest and best-preserved buffalo jumps in North America. For at least 5,000 years, the Blackfoot people came here to stage massive fall hunts. At the interpretive centre, older children can discover all the remarkable details, from the pre-hunt ceremonies and careful preparation of the drive lanes through to the preparation of the meat after the dramatic kill at the cliff face. There's plenty of other fascinating information about the Blackfoot people and their culture; ancient legends are projected onto boulders as visitors walk by and one popular exhibit lets kids test their knowledge of the stone tools used by First Nations peoples.

SEASONS AND TIMES

→ Summer (mid-May—mid-Sept): Daily, 9 am—6 pm.
Winter: Daily, 10 am—5 pm.

COST

→ Adults $6.50, seniors $5.50, youths (7 to 17) $3, under 7 free, families $15.

GETTING THERE

→ By car, take 9th Ave. east to 1st St. S.E. (its name changes to Macleod Trail, then to Hwy. 2) and go south. Continue to Hwy. 785 and turn west. Drive 18 kilometres to the Interpretive Centre. Free parking on site. About two hours from the Calgary Tower.

NEARBY

→ The Fort: Museum of the North West Mounted Police, Live Wild Horse Show and Buffalo Chase.

COMMENT

→ Plan a 3-hour visit.

Also popular is the 200-metre Cliff Top Trail that leads to a spot overlooking the ancient kill site: the view is spectacular. In summer, energetic youngsters will also want to take an hour to tour the lower trail. Here beneath the escarpment, the buffalo meat was prepared and preserved. Pick up a brochure at the information desk before you go. Various points of interest are marked.

When kids get hungry, head to the cafeteria (open in summer only) for some buffalo burgers or more mundane fare. The gift shop is stocked with arts and crafts and souvenir items. Special events and programs include teepee camping packages complete with legends around the campfire, games, guided hikes and interpretive programs.

Riding in the Rockies
WARNER GUIDING AND OUTFITTING

132 BANFF AVE.
BANFF
(403) 762-4551
WWW.HORSEBACK.COM

Warner has 37 years in the horseback riding business and 300 horses to take you and your family on excursions and backcountry rides in one of North America's most beautiful parks. Winter, summer, spring or fall a horsey adventure awaits. In winter, the company offers sleigh rides every day of the week in Banff, every hour of the day from 10 am to 8 pm. In spring, summer and fall, Mountain Morning Breakfast Rides take you by the Sundance Canyon trail and include a hearty steak and egg breakfast. The Explorer Day Ride is a popular ramble through the Spray River Valley and fills your innards with a steak and bean lunch, as well. The Covered Wagon Cookout allows kids to travel like the Western settlers and eat like they did, too.

There are other options. Two to six-day expeditions are this outfit's specialty, with wilderness tenting, outdoor dining and remote lodges adding to the experience. For the multi-day excursions, make sure you either bring all the right gear from home or rent it ahead of time through Performance Ski and Sport at (403) 762-8222.

☞ Seasons and Times

➛ Year-round: Daily. Reservations are required for all rides.
Mountain Morning: Daily, 9 am—noon.
Explorer: Daily, 9:30 am—4:30 pm.
Covered Wagon: Daily, 11 am—2 pm.
Bow River Ride (one hour): Daily departures on the hour 9 am—5 pm.
Sundance Loop (two hours): Daily departures at 10 am, noon, 2 pm and 4 pm.

☞ Cost

➛ Per person: Mountain Morning $61, Explorer $115, Covered Wagon $51, Bow River Ride $25, Sundance Loop $44.
For multi-day rides, prices range from $283 per person for two days at Sundance Lodge to $963 per person for a six-day backcountry lodge ride.

☞ Getting There

➛ Take Centre St. north to 16th Ave. and turn west, driving along 16th (which turns into Hwy. 1) to the town of Banff. Some rides depart from Martin Stables and some from the Banff Springs Hotel Corral; find out where to meet your guide. To get to the Banff Springs Hotel, follow Banff Ave. over the bridge and veer left onto Spray Ave. The hotel is at the end. Park in the hotel's pay parking lot. To get to Martin Stables, follow Banff Ave. over the bridge and turn right onto Cave Ave. Watch for the Recreation Grounds on your right. Martin Stables is at the end of the Recreation Grounds road. Free parking. About 90 minutes from the Calgary Tower.

☞ **Similar Attractions**

→ **Anderson Valley Ranch, Cremona** • (403) 637-3737

→ **Boundary Ranch, Kananaskis Village** • (403) 591-7171

→ **Brewster Lake Louise Stables** Lake Louise • (403) 762-5454

→ **Kananaskis Guest Ranch & Lake Louise Stables & Dance Barn**
(403) 265-7094

→ **Mirage Adventure Tours Ltd. Kananaskis Village**
(403) 678-4919 or 1-888-312-7238

→ **Timberline Tours**
Lake Louise • (403) 522-3743.

Going to the Dogs
DOGSLEDDING IN THE ROCKIES

Dogsledding is the oldest form of winter travel in Canada, originating with the First Nations peoples and Inuit who first settled this country. If you and your family have ever yearned to travel by canine, wrap everyone up warmly, whisk them out to the country and load them onto a sled. Your professional dogsledder hosts will tell you what to expect and (sometimes) how to drive a team; the young and the less ambitious can simply sit on the sled and let the knowledgeable guide do the work. Then, you're all off, gliding through the snow behind a bunch of snappy, happy dogs that live for this stuff. While there are dogsledding operations all over rural Alberta, we've just listed those in the Rockies because they're a more obvious destination for Calgarians. Ski-joering, a relatively new activity where participants wear cross-country skis and the dogs do the pulling, is offered by some of the following outfits. Please note that dogsled trips are dependent on reasonable weather and, of course, snow.

Kingmik Expeditions and Dog Sled Tours

LAKE LOUISE
(403) 522-3525 OR 1-877-919-7779

Complete winter and spring dogsled tours ranging from 30 minutes to five days. Families usually choose the half-hour dogsled tour on the old 1A Highway ($80 per sled), or the three-hour trip down to the Great Divide, on the Alberta-B.C. border ($300 per sled). Each sled fits two adults, a small child and a musher guide. The dogsleds generally run from early November until late April. Ski tours and snowshoe options are also available.

Snowy Owl Sled Tours

CANMORE
(403) 678-4369

Dogsled adventures ranging from two hours to overnight trips in Kananaskis Country. There's also snowshoeing, igloo building and cross-country skiing. All ages are welcome; however, young children on sleds must be chaperoned by an adult. Kids ten and up can be taught how to drive. Scouts, Guides and other groups are welcome. $45 for two hours for children eight and under, $65 for those over eight. Each sled holds a maximum of three.

Mountain Mushers Dog Sled Co.

BANFF
(403) 762-3647

A variety of half-day to multi-day dogsled expeditions in Banff National Park.

Mad Dogs and Englishmen

EXSHAW
(403) 678-0200

Escorted dogsled trips and ski-joering tours throughout Kananaskis. Trips range from one hour to multi-day.

Howling Dog

CANMORE
(403) 678-9588 OR 1-877-364-7533

Offers two-hour to multi-day trips, moonlight rides, ice fishing by dogsled and a snowshoe safari.

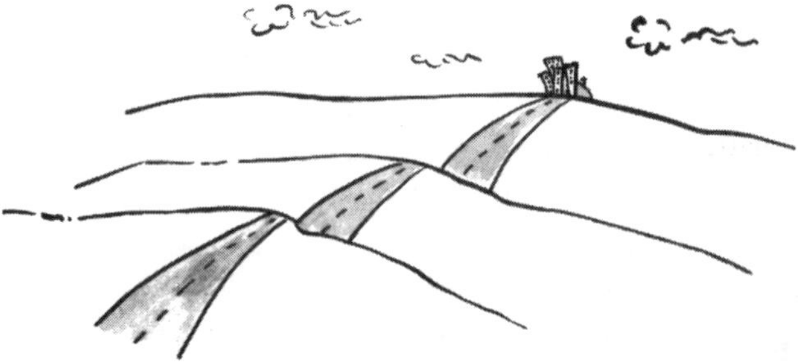

Scale Mountain Peaks
SULPHUR MOUNTAIN GONDOLA

TOP OF SULPHUR MOUNTAIN
BANFF
(403) 762-5438
WWW.BANFFGONDOLA.COM

When the day is clear there are few more beautiful vantage points than the peak of Sulphur Mountain, 2,281 metres above sea level. The truly adventurous may clamber up this enormous pile of rock, but for families the best way to get to what feels like the top of the world is the Sulphur Mountain Gondola. First of all, there are the gentle thrills provided by the ride up as you and your kids look through the windows and see how high you are. Then there are the various hikes along the ridge of the mountain. Bring a camera and dress warmly. It can get very windy up there.

Children will probably be most interested in the self-guided walkway to Sanson's Peak, where interpretive signs explain

☞ SEASONS AND TIMES
➛ Times change monthly, but the gondola runs between 9:30 am and 4:30 pm (Jan—Nov). Visit the Web site or call the number above for details. The Panorama Room is open in summer only. Reservations are not required at the restaurants.

☞ COST
➛ Adults $16, children (6 to 15) $8, under 6 free.

☞ GETTING THERE
➛ Take Centre St. north, turning west onto 16th Ave. (which becomes Hwy. 1) and following it to the Lake Minnewanka/Banff turnoff. Turn south into Banff and follow Banff Ave. over the bridge. Turn left onto Spray Ave. and then take your first right onto Mountain Ave., following the signs to the gondola parking, which is free. About 90 minutes from the Calgary Tower.

☞ NEARBY
➛ Banff Upper Hot Springs, Banff Springs Hotel.

> ☞ **COMMENT**
> ➛ If you want a taste of the visual meal you'll be getting, check out the Web site, where a live WebCam updates the view from Sulphur Mountain every ten minutes.

what you are seeing and how to tell the difference between mountain sheep and mountain goats. And then, of course, there's the 360-degree view.

This well-maintained sight is much more than the sum of its parts. Look around outdoors, then look around some more from the cafeteria-service Summit Restaurant or the buffet-service Panorama or one of the three observation decks. Browse through the gift shop in the Summit Complex. You can stay as long as the gondola is running, unless you relish the thought of an extremely long, steep walk down.

Powder Perfect
SKI THE ROCKIES

The heady experience of skiing some of the most gorgeous and exciting mountain runs in the world is a Calgarian's birthright. It's not cheap, mind you. But if cruising down a long, sweet slope or attacking a heavily-moguled vertical drop appeals to your family, you have nothing but fabulous choices. Equip everyone with goggles, hats, warm jackets and socks and wind-proof gloves because no matter how balmy it may be when you set out from Calgary, the weather could be cold and windy out of town at a high altitude. Remember, skiing in restricted areas in the Rockies is not only against the rules but also extremely dangerous. All prices listed below are full-day rates.

Banff Mount Norquay

BANFF
(403) 762-4421
WWW.BANFFNORQUAY.COM

Well-groomed, uncrowded trails, a handsome lodge and Banff's only night skiing, all ten minutes from the townsite of Banff. Norquay's ski and snowboard school serves kids ages three and up. Rentals available. Wild Child Weekend Warriors Kids Camps run on weekends and other camps run during the school holidays around Christmas and Easter.

☞ Early Dec—mid Apr.

☞ Adults $39, seniors (55 and up), youths and students (with ID) $33, children (6 to 12) $15, under 6 free with purchase of full-price ticket. Afternoon, evening, multi-day and hourly rates available. Also season's passes.

☞ Take Centre St. north and turn west onto 16th Ave. (which turns into Hwy. 1). Drive west on Hwy. 1 past the Banff/Lake Minnewanka turnoff and turn north onto the Mount Norquay turnoff. Follow the signs to the resort. Free parking. About 75 minutes from the Calgary Tower.

Banff Sunshine Village

BANFF
1-877-542-2633
WWW.SKIBANFF.COM

All-natural snow is Sunshine's claim to fame, more than 10 metres of it per year. Sunshine also happens to be the loftiest ski resort in the Canadian Rockies. Skiers and 'boarders flock to this site 15 minutes from the town of Banff, which offers three mountains, three high-speed quads and the only ski-in, ski-out hotel in the park. Mount Standish has improved its snowboard park to entice enthusiasts. Lessons, rentals and various kid-focused programs are available.

☞ Early Nov—late May, daily. Gondola opens at 8 am; ski runs are open from 9 am to 4 pm.

☞ Gondola and ski hill: Adults $50, seniors (65 and up) and students (13 to 25 with ID) $39, children (6 to 12) $15, under 6 free. Afternoon and multi-day passes available.
Gondola only: Adults, seniors and students $15, children $10. Multi-day passes available.

☞ From Centre St. north turn west onto 16th Ave. (which turns into Hwy. 1) and drive past the Banff turnoff for eight kilometres to the Sunshine turnoff. Follow the signs to the free parking lot. Just under two hours from the Calgary Tower.

Fortress

KANANASKIS
(403) 591-7108 OR 1-800-258-7669
WWW.SKIFORTRESS.COM

Fortress is closer to Calgary than Banff because it's located in K-country, 75 minutes west of the city. It's a casual resort that prides itself on wide-open mountain runs, challenging hills (it is, after all, the training site of the Canadian Freestyle Team) and natural half-pipes for snowboarders. Fortress is open in the summer for hiking and mountain biking, although the lifts do not run daily.

☞ Early Nov—late Apr. Chairlift: Mon—Fri, 9 am—4 pm; Sat—Sun, 8:30 am—4 pm.

☞ Adults $29.75, seniors (65 and up), youths (13 to 17) and students (18 to 25 with ID) $22, children (6 to 12) $12, under 6 free. Half-day, afternoon, multi-day and group rates are available.

☞ Take Centre St. north to 16th Ave. and turn west, following 16th Ave. (which turns into Hwy. 1) west until you see the Kananaskis Country sign. Turn south onto Hwy. 40 and follow it for about 40 minutes, watching for the Fortress signs. Free parking on site. About 75 minutes from the Calgary Tower.

Lake Louise

LAKE LOUISE
(403) 522-3555 OR 1-800-258-7669
WWW.SKILOUISE.COM

Louise is Canada's largest single ski area, one of its most scenic and among the top 15 destinations in the world for downhill skiers, according to *Ski Magazine*. It boasts more than 28 square kilometres of ski-able terrain over four mountain faces with over 105 named runs as well as thousands of hectares of open bowl skiing. Snowmaking equipment ensures a six-month ski season. Kids' programs are available. In the summertime, take a trip through the skies on the high-speed Lake Louise Sightseeing Gondola and enjoy beautiful views of wildflowers and natural springs. The 14-minute ride up Mount Whitehorn gets you up to 2,000 metres. At the top of the gondola is Whitehorn Lodge, where you can grab a snack, shop at the gift store and inspect the nature centre. The Observation Deck allows you to gaze over the magnificent Bow Valley.

☞ Skiing: Early Nov—early May, daily, 9 am—4 pm.
Gondola: Early June—late Sept, daily, 8 am—6 pm (starts at 9 am in Sept).

☞ Adults (18 to 64) $53, seniors (65 and up), students (18 to 24 with ID) and youths (13 to 17) $42, children (6 to 12) $15. Half-day, afternoon, late-day, Louise Card rates available.
Gondola (summer): Adults $11, seniors and students $10, youths (6 to 15) $8, under 6 free.

☞ Take Centre St. north to 16th Ave. and turn west, following 16th Ave. (which becomes Hwy. 1) about 60 kilometres past the town of Banff. Watch for the Lake Louise turnoff; take it and then follow the signs to the ski resort. Free parking. About two hours from the Calgary Tower.

Other Places that are Farther Afield

Buffalo Nations Luxton Museum

1 Birch Ave.
Banff
(403) 762-2388
http://collections.ic.gc.ca/luxton/

The Buffalo Nations Luxton Museum allows kids to explore the heritage of the Indians of the Northern Plains and Canadian Rockies. Housed in a remarkable fort-like log building, this handsome museum should not be overlooked. Exhibits include costumes and everyday clothing decorated with intricate porcupine quill designs, traditional hunting equipment and dioramas showing such fascinating rituals as the Buffalo Jump and the Sun Dance. Teepees, a sweat lodge and examples of the animals hunted by Canada's first peoples help round out the museum's displays. During the summer, traditional and contemporary First Nations' cultural activities are presented live.

☞ May—mid-Oct, daily, 9 am—7 pm.
Mid-Oct—May, daily, 1 pm—5 pm.

☞ Adults $6, seniors $4, children (6 to 18) $2.50, under 6 free, families $13.

☞ Take Centre St. north to 16th Ave. and turn west. Follow 16th (which turns into Hwy. 1) to the Banff/Lake Minnewanka turnoff and turn south, into the town of Banff. Follow Banff Ave. just across the bridge and immediately turn right onto Birch Ave. or Cave Ave. The museum is between the two avenues. Free parking in the museum lot. About 90 minutes from the Calgary Tower.

Cave and Basin National Historic Site

311 CAVE AVE.
BANFF
(403) 762-1566
WWW.WORLDWEB.COM/PARKSCANADA-BANFF

When William McCardell, his brother Tom and their partner Frank McCabe stumbled on this mist-filled site back in 1883, the mountain's natural hot springs inspired them to dream of a place where people would come from all over the world to soak and revitalize themselves. Their money-making notion was soon stymied by the government of Canada, which decided to turn the lands around the Cave and Basin into a national park with its own warm mineral springs pool. These days, the pool at the Cave and Basin is no longer open to swimmers. But visitors still come to see the intriguing on-site museum. The warm water that used to feed the swimming pool now feeds the nearby marsh, creating an inviting environment for all kinds of plant and animal life, including a snail that exists nowhere else on earth. Delicate orchids, garter snakes, wild animals and most of Banff's native birds can be found here. Check out the museum and explore its history, but do also take time for a walk along the Marsh Trail.

☞ Late May—late Sept, daily, 9 am—6 pm.
Oct—late May, weekdays, 11 am—4 pm; Sat—Sun, 9:30 am—5 pm.

☞ Adults $2.50, seniors $2, youths $1.50, families $5.75.

☞ Take Centre St. north to 16th Ave. and turn west, following 16th Ave. (which turns into Hwy. 1) to the Banff turnoff. Follow Banff Ave. over the bridge and turn right onto Cave Ave. Follow the signs to the Cave and Basin parking lot, which will be on your left. About 90 minutes from the Calgary Tower.

Wild Rapids Water Slide

5104 Lakeshore Dr.
Sylvan Lake
(403) 887-3636

With 16 fun-filled rides, Wild Rapids Water Slide offers up summertime treats to every member of the family. While speed demons rocket down one of two speed slides or test their mettle on Canada's first Sidewinder, less adventurous family members can enjoy one of four twister slides. There are also two Mammoth River inner tube rides and a large hot pool for quiet basking. Little tykes have their own pint-size paradise—a warm water wading pool complete with two squirting frogs and four small slides. There are two concession stands and a picnic area on site. If you'd rather lie around on the beach, visit Sylvan Lake, where you can rent jet skis, pedal boats and windsurfing equipment.

☞ Waterslides: Early June—mid-June, weekends, 11 am—6 pm; late June—Labour Day, daily, 11 am—7 pm.

☞ Waterslides: Over 122 cm $19.95, under 122 cm $15.95, tots 2 and under free.
Public beach: Free.

☞ By car, take 9th Ave. east to Macleod Trail and go north. Turn east on 5th Ave. and go over the overpass. Stay to the right and head east on Memorial Dr. At Deerfoot Trail (its name changes to Hwy. 2) head north to Red Deer and take Hwy. 11A (it becomes Lakeshore Dr. at Sylvan Lake) east to the waterslides. Pay parking on site ($3.50 per day). About two hours from the Calgary Tower.

White Mountain Adventures

CANMORE
(403) 678-4099 OR 1-800-408-0005
WWW.CANADIANNATUREGUIDES.COM

White Mountain Adventures offers many intriguing trips into the wilderness that families (adults and children over seven) can go on. In winter, sign up for the Johnston Canyon ice walks and gaze at waterfalls frozen into fabulous shapes. Travel along the bottom of the canyon and over suspended catwalks to the Twin Pools and the Upper Falls amphitheatre. There are also snowshoeing trips to see wildlife. Or, participate in Night Tracks, where your guide leads you on an adventure through snowy forests and along icy rivers in the evening; sometimes the Northern Lights make an appearance.

In summer, White Mountain takes visitors up to Sunshine Meadows for a gander at high-altitude plants, animals and ecosystems. The Flowers and Colours hike, ideal for families, takes you through the ever-changing flora of the Rockies. Certified guides are provided with each trip. You can also take the shuttle up and hike on your own, if you prefer, though you must keep to the pathways to avoid injuring fragile plants.

☞ Call White Mountain Adventures or visit their Web site for the exact dates and times of the tours.

☞ Prices vary, but generally range from $18 to $45 for adults and $18 to $25 for children, depending on the tour. Special equipment and transportation included.

☞ Take Centre St. north to 16th Ave. and turn west onto 16th (which becomes Hwy. 1) and continue west to Banff National Park or Lake Louise. If you're taking the shuttle from the Sunshine parking lot, you can park there for free. If your destination is Sunshine, it's just under two hours from the Calgary Tower, if Banff, 90 minutes, if Lake Louise, two hours.

12 Months of Fun
DIRECTORY OF EVENTS

JANUARY

To early January
TransAlta's Wildlights
Calgary Zoo & Botanical Gardens
Calgary
(403) 232-9300

Late January
Banff/Lake Louise Winter Festival
Banff and Lake Louise
(403) 762-8421

Late January
Canmore Winterfest
Canmore
(403) 678-1295

FEBRUARY

Early February
Winter Fun Fest
Cypress Hills
(403) 893-3777

Early to late February
Calgary Winter Festival
Calgary
(403) 543-5480

MARCH

Mid-March
Rough Stock
Stampede Corral
Calgary
1-800-661-1260

APRIL

Early April
Easter Parade
17th Ave. S.W.
Calgary
(403) 245-1703

Mid-April to late April
Kiwanis Festival
Calgary
(403) 283-6009

Late April
Aggie Days—Family Fun Day
Stampede Park
Calgary
(403) 261-9316

Late April
Mom & Tots Fair
Stampede Park
Calgary
(403) 261-0101

Late April
Easter Egg-Stravaganza
Calgary Zoo
Calgary
(403) 232-9300

Late April
Banff Celebration of Mountain Heritage
(Native and cowboy exhibits, pack-horse competition and dance)
Banff
(403) 762-8421

MAY

Early May
Mother's Day Brunch
Calgary Zoo & Botanical Gardens
(403) 232-9300

Late May
Calgary International Children's Festival
Arts Centre
Calgary
(403) 294-7414

Last weekend in May
Fourth Street Lilac Festival
Calgary
(403) 229-0902

JUNE

Early June
The National
Spruce Meadows
(403) 974-4200
www.sprucemeadows.com

Early June
Bloomfest
Calgary Zoo & Botanical Gardens
(403) 232-9300

Early June
Railway Days
Heritage Park
(403) 259-1900

Early June to late August
Banff Festival of the Arts
Banff Centre
Banff
(403) 762-6300

Mid-June
Carifest Caribbean Festival
Various venues around Calgary
(403) 292-0310

Mid-June
Midsummer Magic
Calgary Zoo & Botanical Gardens
Calgary
(403) 232-9300

Father's Day
Kite Day
South Glenmore Park
Calgary
(403) 221-3530

Father's Day
Father's Day Barbecue
Calgary Zoo & Botanical Gardens
Calgary
(403) 232-9300

Father's Day
Heritage Park
Calgary
(403) 259-1900

Late June
Calgary International Jazz Festival
Various venues around Calgary
(403) 249-1119

Late June to early July
The Canadian Badlands Passion Play
Drumheller
(403) 823-7750

Late June to early July
Canada One (Show Jumping)
Spruce Meadows
(403) 974-4200

JULY

Banff Festival of the Arts
Banff Centre
Banff
(403) 762-6300

To early July
The Canadian Badlands Passion Play
Drumheller
(403) 823-7750

To early July
Canada One (Show Jumping)
Spruce Meadows
(403) 974-4200

Canada Day celebrations in Calgary
Prince's Island Park
(403) 268-3888
Calgary Zoo • (403) 232-9300
Heritage Park • (403) 259-1900
Fort Calgary Historic Park
(403) 290-1875

Early July to mid-August
Shakespeare in the Park
Prince's Island Park
Calgary
(403) 240-6908

Early July to mid-August
Untamed Tuesdays
Calgary Zoo & Botanical Gardens
Calgary
(403) 232-9300

Early July to late August
Jazzoo
Calgary Zoo & Botanical Gardens
Calgary
(403) 232-9300

Mid-July
The North American (Show Jumping)
Spruce Meadows
(403) 974-4200

Mid-July
The Calgary Stampede
Stampede Park and other places around town
Calgary
(403) 261-0101

Mid-July
Buffalo Days Pow Wow and Tipi Village
Head Smashed-In Buffalo Jump
Fort Macleod
(403) 553-2731

Late July
Calgary Folk Festival
Various venues around Calgary
(403) 233-0904
www.calgaryfolkfest.com

Late July
Alberta Dragon Boat Races
Glenmore Reservoir
(403) 216-0145

Late July
Sun & Salsa
Kensington (Louise Crossing) Area
(403) 283-4810

Late July
Tsuu T'ina Nation Rodeo
Tsuu T'ina Reserve
(403) 281-4455

Late July
Big Valley Country Music Jamboree
Camrose
(403) 672-0224 or 1-888-404-1234

Late July
Calgary Summer Festival of Arts and Crafts
Canada Olympic Park
Calgary
(403) 286-2632

AUGUST

Early August
Hayshaker Days
Heritage Park
Calgary
(403) 259-1900

Early August
Heritage Family Festival
Heritage Park
Calgary
(403) 259-1900

Early August
Heritage Days Folk Festival
Canmore
(403) 678-2524

To mid-August
Shakespeare in the Park
Prince's Island Park
Calgary
(403) 240-6908

To mid-August
Untamed Tuesdays
Calgary Zoo & Botanical Gardens
Calgary
(403) 232-9300

Mid-August
Afrikadey!
Various locations around town
Calgary
(403) 234-9110
www.afrikadey.org

To late August
Banff Festival of the Arts
Banff Centre
Banff
(403) 762-6300

To late August
Jazzoo
Calgary Zoo & Botanical Gardens
Calgary
(403) 232-9300

Late August
Shady Grove Bluegrass Music Festival
Broadway Farm
High River
(403) 652-5550

Late August
Hispanic Festival
Various locations around town
Calgary
(403) 271-2744
www.hispanicarts.com

SEPTEMBER

Early September
Canmore Highland Games
Canmore
(403) 678-9454

Early September
Barbecue on the Bow
Prince's Island
Calgary
(403) 225-1913

Early September
Fall Fair
Heritage Park
Calgary
(403) 259-1900

Early September
Fall Harvest Festival
Heritage Park
Calgary
(403) 259-1900

Early September to mid-September
The Masters (Show Jumping)
Spruce Meadows
Calgary
(403) 974-4200

Late September to early October
Calgary International Film Festival
Plaza Theatre
Calgary
(403) 283-1490
www.calgaryfilm.com/about.html

Late September to early October
Octoberwest
Heritage Park
Calgary
(403) 259-1910

OCTOBER

To early October
Calgary International Film Festival
Plaza Theatre
Calgary
(403) 283-1490
www.calgaryfilm.com/about.html

To early October
Octoberwest
Heritage Park
Calgary
(403) 259-1910

Early October
World's Largest Garage Sale
Stampede Park
Calgary
(403) 261-0101

Early October
Thank You Weekend
Heritage Park
Calgary
(403) 259-1910

Late October
Boo at the Zoo
Calgary Zoo & Botanical Gardens
Calgary
(403) 232-9300

Late October
Junior League Art and Craft Fair
Stampede Park
Calgary
(403) 261-0101 or
1-800-661-1260

NOVEMBER

Early November
Banff Festival of Mountain Films
Banff Centre
Banff
(403) 571-1820

November 11
Remembrance Day Activities
Museum of the Regiments
Calgary
(403) 974-2850

Mid-November
Festival of Trees
Stampede Park
Calgary
(403) 261-0101

Late November
Art Market
Calgary Convention Centre
Calgary
(403) 762-2345

Late November to early January
TransAlta's Wildlights
Calgary Zoo & Botanical Gardens
Calgary
(403) 232-9300

Late November
Kennel and Obedience Show
Stampede Park
(403) 261-0101

Late November to late December
Twelve Days of Christmas
Heritage Park
(403) 259-1910
www.heritagepark.ab.ca

DECEMBER

TransAlta's Wildlights
Calgary Zoo & Botanical Gardens
Calgary
(403) 232-9300

Early to late December
Lions Club Festival of Lights
Confederation Park
Calgary
(403) 273-5466

Early December
Festival of Crafts
Stampede Park
(403) 261-0101

Early December
Santa Claus Parade
Downtown Calgary
(403) 215-1570
www.downtowncalgary.com

Early December to late December
The Nutcracker
Jubilee Auditorium
Calgary
(403) 245-4222

To late December
Twelve Days of Christmas
Heritage Park
(403) 259-1910
www.heritagepark.ab.ca

INDEX

Workshops/Camps/Programs